MAKING it HAPPEN

A Non-Technical Guide to Project Management

MACKENZIE KYLE

JOHN WILEY & SONS CANADA, LTD

Toronto • New York • Chichester • Weinheim • Brisbane • Singapore

Copyright © 1998 by Mackenzie Kyle

John Wiley & Sons Canada Limited
22 Worcester Road
Etobicoke, Ontario
M9W 1L1

Canadian Cataloguing in Publication Data
Kyle, Mackenzie, 1966–
   Making it happen : a non-technical guide to project management

ISBN 0-471-64234-7

1. Industrial project management. I. Title.

HD69.P75K95 1998   658.4'04   C98-931280-1

Production Credits
Cover & text design: JAQ, RGD
Printer: Tri-Graphic Printing

Printed in Canada

10 9 8 7 6 5 4 3

Contents

Preface

This book has two things to offer you as a reader.

The first is a unique and superior approach to the discipline of project management. Much is known about projects (and vastly more is written), but not much is widely understood. The ideas presented here were refined over many years by individuals who have spent their careers in the field, making the concepts of the management sciences work. This useful approach was not developed without cost and frustration, and there is a great deal contained here that you will find nowhere else.

The second is the manner in which the ideas are conveyed. Learning should always be an adventure, although sometimes it is not. If you've ever stumbled through a dry textbook, struggling to make important information stick in your brain, you'll appreciate the alternative approach taken by this book. Without the excitement generated by discovery, it is very hard to retain, let alone implement, new ideas.

Making learning interesting has been one of the greatest challenges of my job. My colleagues and I have developed a number of techniques for doing this, and in the course of our work, experienced a great deal of success in improving how companies operate. In early 1993, I decided to take the approach that became the following story. This is not another attempt to make a simple subject complex, nor to make a complex subject *seem* simple. It is a demonstration of how simple it really is.

If you choose this book to assist you in your learning adventure, you will follow the "real life" journey of discovery of a person not unlike yourself, and see the application of new and powerful ideas to the discipline of making things happen.

Mackenzie Kyle
Vancouver, British Columbia
April 1998

Part One

Genesis

1

Sink or Swim

"So you see, we'll need a work breakdown structure almost immediately," he said.

"I see," I said. I didn't.

"Ralph is also asking for earned value cost analysis, and he wants you to keep the scope flexible, understand?" he asked me.

"I understand," I said. I didn't.

"And he wants self-empowered work teams running the show on this one," he continued.

"Got it," I said, pretending to take notes. I didn't have a clue what he was talking about.

"And the whole thing has to be part of our new Total Quality Management initiative," he said.

I groaned. This was the last straw. Now was the time to get off this boat. "I'm not sure you have the right person for the job, Stu."

I could tell by the way he looked at me that this was not what he wanted to hear. I prepared myself for his response, praying my lack of enthusiasm would get me bounced off the project team.

I didn't hold out much hope. Stu Barnes is the vice-president of Operations at Hyler Recreation Systems Inc., and my boss. Me, I'm Will Campbell, and I'm in charge of Hyler's Information Systems, or IS, group. Stu and I had worked together for almost three years by the time we had this conversation, and we knew each other pretty well. Although Stu looked and talked like a Marine Drill Sergeant (which is exactly what he used to be), he is the best boss I have ever had. While this was a good thing most of the time, it also meant that Stu was used to me whining.

"Look, Will," he started in, "you know how I feel about all this stuff, but Ralph is the boss, and we all know that Ralph has his sights set on much bigger things than Hyler. If that means riding the crest of whatever wave comes rolling in from head office, that is exactly what he'll do. And that means that's exactly what we'll do."

Ralph Borsellino is the president of Hyler Recreation and at 34, the youngest president ever. The top brass at Mantec, our parent company, was very impressed with Ralph, and word was that he was on his way up in the organization.

Inwardly, I groaned again. Stu was right. If Ralph wanted it, that is the way it would be.

The Company

The meeting had not started out badly. "So what we have here," Stu had been telling me, "is a major opportunity to complement our existing product line, and you know how they love that kind of thing at head office in Denver. Not only will it create new customers, but if our experience is anything like what they've seen in Europe, it will lead to more sales of our existing products further down the line."

This was exciting news. Although I had spent the last 18 months in the Information Systems area, Hyler was a small organization and everyone knew the ground rules. Our company was just a stop-over for the up-and-coming movers and shakers at Mantec. Innovation leading to expanded sales was a sure ticket for promotion out of

Hyler. But to put all of that in context, I should tell you a little bit about the organization.

Andrew Hyler started the company during the war to make life boats and life rafts for the U.S. Navy. He located his operation in Enderby, Oregon, just outside Portland. Like many war-time industrialists with a guaranteed demand and price, he was successful. When the war ended and new military contracts were not forthcoming, Andrew decided to go on making boats, but now they would be pleasure boats. Everyone called him crazy, especially since he lived way out in Oregon, where there were not a lot of people.

Old Andrew must have seen what was coming because he did very well for himself. After the war, just about all forms of recreation became popular and boating was no exception. Since Hyler was the only manufacturer on the West Coast, he had a definite competitive advantage. Not only did he build better boats than they made back East, he could sell them cheaper because his shipping costs were a fraction of the competition's. He had such a grip on the market that none of the Eastern manufacturers even bothered to open up a West Coast plant. When aluminum boats became popular, Andrew was well positioned to scoop that market too.

By the time the sixties rolled around, Andrew Hyler was getting on and he no longer wanted the day-to-day hassles of running a business. In 1967 he sold the company to Mantec Corporation, a major conglomerate whose holdings included oil and gas fields, refineries, pulp mills, trucking companies, and vast amounts of real estate. The purchase of a boat plant was the final step in an elaborate plan that the Mantec executives had worked out. Hyler was to be a training ground for developing managers. "Trainees" could make their mistakes and learn at Hyler, where the stakes were small, before moving on to bigger and better things within the parent corporation. To this day, all of Mantec's top executives, and the heads of most of its subsidiaries, have spent time at Hyler.

This means that managers who come through our company have high expectations placed on them, which is probably why Hyler has led the field in recreational boating on the West Coast for the last 25 years. The company now has sales approaching $40 million, and in addition to aluminum boats (which are a decreasing portion of our business), we make several models of windsurfers, sailboats, boat trailers, dinghies, and sails. Our last big product line expansion was into personal floatation devices. That was the brainchild of the former vice-president of Marketing, and it did so well that she is now president of one of Mantec's huge box companies in Texas.

So what Stu was saying about this new product was bound to make a guy like Ralph Borsellino happy.

The New Product

Stu continued to give me details. "The really exciting thing is that this new product looks like it will overcome the windsurfing Resistance Factor."

The famed Resistance Factor. This was news, indeed! RF, as we called it, was Hyler's term for people's reluctance to take up windsurfing (at least their resistance to get into it enough so that they would actually purchase their own windsurfer, ideally from us).

My first project as head of Information Systems had been to oversee a consumer survey about a variety of recreational activities. The survey produced some interesting information about how people choose to recreate, and about windsurfing in particular. Although everyone has seen the pros on TV skimming across the waves and doing spectacular acrobatics, windsurfing is not an easy sport for the average beginner. Anyone who has tried it knows it can even be a little frustrating. Unfortunately, frustrated beginners rarely become windsurfer owners, hence the RF. Ever since that survey, we've been looking for ways to overcome that problem. To get comparative data, we surveyed several sports, not just windsurfing. Downhill skiing scored very high for the beginner. Even the first time out, novices can get their skis pointed downhill and can, in a manner of speaking, ski. With windsurfing, many of the people surveyed reported that they couldn't even pull the sail up the first time that they went out. And somehow, windsurfing just isn't all that much fun without the sail.

Interested now, I said, "So don't keep me waiting, Stu, tell me about it. Have you got a new windsurfer design or what?"

"In fact," Stu said, "the Europeans have a new design. Water-Trends out of Germany introduced a new product late this summer. I've seen it, and I think it can be very successful over here."

"So what does it look like?" I asked, "And how does it overcome the RF?"

Stu reached into his desk and pulled out a sketch. "It's essentially a cross between a small sailboat and a regular windsurfer," he said as he put the drawing on the desk in front of me.

The sketch showed a board that looked like a regular windsurfer, but it appeared broader, and had a seat with a back set into its surface. A women was sitting in the seat, her legs extended, her feet resting against a horizontal bar close to the front. The mast sat forward of the foot rest, rose about four feet, and had a boom that extended back and stopped a couple feet from her chest. The sail was a bit on the small side compared to a windsurfer.

"You see," Stu was saying, "the feet control the rudder with that horizontal bar there, and you have a sheet in each hand to control the sail." Being a non-sailor, I always have to remember that sheets are ropes attached to the boom used to control sails.

"I don't get it," I said. "How is this better than a windsurfer?"

"I was hoping you'd ask me that," Stu said gleefully. "It combines the best features of both sailboat and windsurfer, and that's how it overcomes the RF."

I was not impressed. "It looks like a water slug to me."

Stu rolled his eyes to the ceiling. "Why am I cursed with vision-less peasants?" Turning back to me he said, "Look, people like wind-surfers for some very simple reasons: They're very portable—you can put them on your car top, they're flexible in the water—you can go fast in very little wind, jump waves, and, if you're very good, do really fancy things like complete loops. They're a lot cheaper than sailboats. But beginners have a hard time with windsurfers.

"On the other hand, a little sailboat is easy for a beginner. It doesn't go too fast, it's easy to steer the thing, and no feats of strength are required. However, a beginner doesn't want to rush out and spend four or five thousand bucks for a sailboat, and then have to tow it around on a trailer, especially if they only use it a few times a year.

"Enter the WindSailor. It's lightweight and portable like the windsurfer, it costs the same or less, and yet it has all the user-friendly features of a small sailboat. There is no heavy sail to lift, they don't go too fast—see how small that sail is—and they're almost impossible to tip. A dagger board drops down between your legs for stability. And if you do tip, an eight year old can get it right side up again. And guess what? After using the WindSailor for a year or two, the consumer wants to move up, either to a proper windsurfer, or to a sailboat. And who do you think will be right there to supply them with that product?" Stu sat back looking very pleased.

"You'd almost think this whole thing was your idea," I said.

"It was," he said, "at least the push to buy the manufacturing license for North America. I saw this baby at a trade show in Europe four months ago."

"Why not just steal the idea and design our own?"

"Will," he said with mock dismay, "How could you think such a thing? Anyway, we don't have time. Our marketing guys say if we're not first into the market with this, we'll lose our edge and it will be doubtful we would ever recover the development cost. Besides, it could take more than a year to get it right. If we buy the rights on this one, we have a known quantity on our hands."

"Yeah," I said, "we know all about it except whether it will sell." I paused, "This is a big risk for you personally. What did Ralph say about it?"

Stu sighed. "Look, kid, I've been at this plant for 15 years, and I've been stalled in this job for the last seven. Ralph is going to be moving on soon. I want that top job. I'm sick of seeing hot shots come in here for a year or two and run this place like they want a promotion. I want control for a few years to make Hyler the kind of place where I want to work. This WindSailor is my ticket."

This was the first Stu had told me about his personal ambition. Not only was Stu the best boss I had ever had, a lot of others felt the same way. Although Hyler was certainly not in any trouble, it could have been a much better place to work. The constant shuffle at the top levels tended to make many of the longer term employees unhappy. Stu had never been tapped for the top job, mostly it seemed, because he was not on his way up within the bigger organization of Mantec.

"Anyway," Stu continued, "you know Ralph. If it looks good, he's 100 percent behind you until it looks bad, at which point it was your idea. If this does go, he'll be promoted and I'll have a shot at his job. If it's a flop, well, I need a change anyway."

My predecessor was one of those people whom Ralph supported 100 percent until things started looking bad. She had developed a great idea about using the IS department as a clearing house for employee feedback. Of course not all of it was positive, and Ralph had started getting nervous about someone other than him knowing the dirty secrets about employee attitudes. She was fired for "poor performance", but everyone knew the real reason.

Stu sighed. "Besides, regardless of promotions or office politics, I happen to think this is what the company should be doing." He stuck his chin out heroically.

Whenever people start to get noble, I get nervous. Doing the "right" thing is nice up until you haven't got a job anymore.

"Well, you know me, Stu," I told him. "I'll support you however I can. I'd love to see you get Ralph's job. What can I do?"

Stu looked at me, and suddenly I felt like a lamb being mentally barbecued by a wolf. He smiled. "I want you to be the Project Manager."

I stared back at him. Project Manager? A hundred objections formed themselves in my mind—I don't know anything about boat design! I know nothing about factory set-up! I'm not an engineer!

The Project Manager

Instead of voicing these thoughts I said, "Okay."

"Good!" he said, clapping his hands together. My feeling of doom deepened.

"Now Ralph did, of course, impose a few conditions. Nothing too serious, nothing we can't work around."

Just what I like. Conditions set by the boss that you have to work around.

"For starters, I'll be the project sponsor, but you'll ultimately have to go to Ralph for spending approval."

"Right," I said. Oh good, I thought, up the bureaucratic ladder to the ultimate control freak before I can spend a dime. That will be fun.

"Ralph wants Al Burton on the project team." Stu looked at me, anticipating some kind of response.

"What!!" I screamed, "That asshole? The last project he was on was a total screw up. What the hell do we need—"

"As you know," Stu interrupted, "TQM was a complete success."

"That project was a disaster!" I retorted.

A year ago, when Total Quality Management was trendy, Ralph had assigned Al Burton to implement it at our plant. Al seemed the logical choice because he was an engineer, was head of Industrial and Production Engineering, and was the only Certified Project Manager at Hyler. Although it was supposed to have taken three months, according to Al, and cost $150,000, it was still going on, in a haphazard way. The bill was now almost $800,000. Since no objective had yet been established, other than to "do things in a quality way", no results had been achieved. Morale in the plant had never been worse.

Stu said, "You and I both know it was and is a dismal failure. But Ralph needed it to be successful, and so it was successful. Putting Al on this team is Ralph's way of having an insider, a spy. Ralph can depend on Al, because Ralph had to make sure TQM and Al's project didn't fail." He sighed. "In this organization, politics are part of everything we do. You'd be stupid to ignore it. Just don't let it affect the success you want to achieve."

I knew that was good advice, but it got so frustrating having to work within those ground rules. I began to pray Al would get hit by a bus.

"You know how Ralph likes jargon," Stu continued, "Well, he picked up a bunch of things from Al's last project that he wants to see on this one."

I readied my pencil and paper.

"Ralph wants you using some project management software to make reporting easier." Wonderful, I thought. More software to learn. "He wants a schedule of milestones by the end of this week. He wants to see it in a Gantt chart format, but he's leaving the choice of the software up to you." Stu added that I had to provide work breakdown structures, earned value costing, TQM integration, and this is where you came into the conversation.

I had survived many projects in the past, but the size of this one made me nervous, not to mention the employment implications. I had a sign in my office that looked like this:

Steps in a Project

1. Enthusiasm
2. Action
3. Consternation
4. Panic
5. Obfuscation
6. Punishment of the innocent
7. Praise and rewards to the non-participants

It was supposed to be humorous, but it rang just a little too true.

I had a vague idea about work breakdown structures, earned value costing, and I had actually tried using Gantt charts for doing scheduling. I had used those tools in one of my university courses, but none of them had helped me much on real projects. And now I felt like I would be needing all the help I could get.

"Why me?" I asked Stu, "Why not Al? He's the certified project manager."

Stu sighed again and stared off into the middle distance. "I want this thing to have a chance of succeeding," The compliment must have shown on my face because he immediately said, "Now don't get a swelled head. You could just as easily screw it up. But I know Al has the wrong approach. He's proved it on every project he's managed here at Hyler. You, on the other hand, have a fighting chance of trying something different, even if out of desperation, and we just might succeed."

As I sat there feeling somewhat deflated, he continued. "I know you, Will, and you don't put a lot of stock in textbooks if you see that it doesn't work in reality. Al believes that if the textbooks say it, it must be right, regardless of whether it actually works."

"So I've got a free rein to do whatever makes it work?"

Stu hedged. "Within reason. You've still got to keep Ralph happy, and there's not much leeway on the money side. But yes, I will try and run interference so you can do whatever works."

That was the last good thing I heard all morning.

2

Grasping the Scope

Before I left his office, Stu provided more details about the Wind-Sailor.

The WindSailor board was made from a relatively new fiberglass resin compound, and because of this the board needed to be painted with a special sealant that required a longer than normal curing time. Since I don't know a great deal about the chemistry of reinforced plastics (or any chemistry at all), this didn't mean much to me until Stu told me that this would place constraints on our manufacturing facility. Specifically, we would have to provide extra warehouse space for the curing process. This space had to be part of, or connected to, the manufacturing space. The boards could not be transported very far, and certainly not outside, after they had been sealed.

According to Leslie Frame in marketing, who had been in Europe working with the WaterTrends people, we expected to sell about 2,600 WindSailors in the first year, at a price of about $1,600 each. Although that meant only a ten percent sales increase at Hyler, Leslie was projecting sales of almost $10 million by the third year. That represented a significant chunk of money for the company.

The Europeans had introduced the WindSailor in only a few geographic areas in late July, having missed their first-of-the-season target date by a wide margin (my ears pricked up when I heard that), so they did not have much marketing data to go on. The response in those selected areas, however, had been impressive. Their initial run of 2,500 boards sold out within four weeks, and they had back orders for next year equal to three-quarters of their production capacity. They were increasing their capacity to meet what they hoped would be an even greater demand next season.

Leslie estimated that by purchasing the North American manufacturing and distribution rights to the WindSailor, Stu had given Hyler a least a full year's head start on any North American competition, and on other European manufacturers who might try to export to our market. Since this was a brand-new product, Leslie figured that this head start would give us market dominance over any competing boards for as much as three years, more if our marketing and promotion efforts were done well.

There was, of course, a catch that Stu seemed almost happy to relate. Leslie and the WaterTrend folks in Germany figured it would take the competition about 16 to 18 months to design, test, and produce a board that would get around the WindSailor patent protection and compete head to head with our product.

"So you see," said Stu, "we have to get our WindSailor into the marketplace before the end of next summer." It was now August. "That leaves you almost ten months. No problem!" He actually reached across the desk and slapped me on the shoulder.

No problem. Design the new facility, build it, buy all the equipment, and get it running properly in less than ten months. As I thought about this, I became even more appreciative of the fact that we were located near Portland, where it does not snow and you can do construction work all year.

Our distribution system always pushes our production dates back earlier than you would expect. Hyler owns only one retail outlet, and it is located at our plant. The rest of our product is sold through a variety of privately owned sporting goods stores. This means our products have to be ready for sale well before the final customer wants to buy them. Distribution time is a reality that has to be factored into all of our production schedules. To get the WindSailor out to the public for, say, the last part of next summer, we would have to have it ready for sale by June. This would allow adequate time to get it out to retailers.

The First Cost Estimate

Stu interrupted my little reverie. "As you might expect," he said, "The Hyler board of directors, in all their wisdom, have already decided how much this project will cost." I hated these pronouncements. We had only a rough idea of what work was needed, and the directors were already telling us what we would be spending, regardless of anything we might discover to the contrary. Based on my experience, I expected we would discover to the contrary. Then there would be hell to pay, even though the board must have pulled the cost estimate out of thin air.

"We have $1 million to spend, not including new equipment costs. Think you can do it for that?"

"Stu," I began, "how am I supposed to answer that question? I just found out about the project 20 minutes ago."

"Good," said Stu, ignoring my protest, "I'll tell Ralph that you can. I wouldn't want to disappoint him."

"Hold on a minute," I said, getting my courage up. "One million may be the board's figure, but I refuse to be caught out on this project like every other one. As soon as I know differently, Ralph is going to have to approve a new budget."

Stu looked at me as if there was a whole world of pain out there that I didn't understand. "Sure, sure," he said. "Whatever it takes.

Just make sure you pass it through me before you go talking to Ralph." He sighed. "You may want to keep yourself pure and clean and out of the office politics, but one of us has to keep an eye on it. In fact, I think you'd better look at me as your political advisor on this one, as well as your sponsor."

That seemed fair enough since his neck was out even more than mine.

"Well," I said, standing up, "I better get going on this thing." I had a last minute thought, "Who will I be coordinating with on the Human Resources end of things?"

Stu just looked at me and didn't say anything.

I prompted him. "You know, with all the new machines, we'll have to hire and train a bunch of people." Stu still didn't say anything and kept on looking at me. I started to get it. "Aw, Stu, "I sounded like a little kid whose bedtime had come half-way into his favorite TV show. "There's a hell of a lot of work here. I don't even know what I'm doing on the manufacturing side!"

Stu finally spoke. "I'm not going to break this into a million little pieces and hope that everything will get done. The whole thing is part of the same big project, and I want it run that way." I must have looked depressed because he added, "You won't be all on your own, you know. With my help you can pull team members from every department, and they'll be doing most of the work in their areas. But I want you coordinating the whole thing."

Resigned, I asked, "For the new systems as well?"

"The whole thing," Stu said. "Except for the marketing campaign and the actual roll-out, which Marketing will handle. I want you to coordinate it all."

Gathering Courage

With those words ringing in my ears, I took my leave and headed back to my office. The more I thought about the whole thing, the more unhappy I was. Not only was this project important for the company, Stu's hopes of promotion were riding on it too. It wasn't that I minded pressure, it was just that projects always seemed to turn out poorly, or with mixed results at best. Hard as I had tried, I had never figured out a way to improve the result.

If my budget was $1 million, Marketing would probably have nearly that amount too. Recreational products are very marketing intensive. Two million dollars was a lot of money for Hyler to invest, and that didn't take into account the increase in operating expenses that would result from this product. Head office would never let Hyler go under, but it would let people's careers get into serious trouble. If things didn't go well, not only would Stu not be getting his promotion, but I would probably want to dust off my resume. All of this hanging on a project. I felt something funny happening in my stomach.

My loyal department staff were not much help, either for my stomach or my lack of knowledge about projects.

"Better dust off the old resume," said Amanda Payton after I told her about my meeting with Stu. Amanda is my second in command in Information Systems, and one of my favorite people at Hyler.

"It sounds like one of those projects that can really go down in flames!" She smiled encouragingly. To reduce her smugness to a more bearable level, I said, "Yes, no question it will be a challenge. But thank God I have you around to help! The project is going to take up a lot of my time over the next ten months, so I'll be needing you to take over my responsibilities on a regular basis. Of course, we won't be getting any extra people to help us here in IS, so you will still have your own stuff to look after." I paused, and then because it didn't sound like enough I added, "And I think I'll be needing your expertise on the project "team" as well. Looks like we'll be spending a few late nights together." I gave her my best "team" smile.

Her smugness transformed into minor depression and I felt a little better. When I told her Ralph had assigned Al Burton to the team, Amanda was not impressed. "Al is going to be a major burden. He does everything by the book. And half the time he has the wrong book!"

I wished that everyone else's opinion of Al was not quite as dismal as mine.

"When are you getting started?" Amanda asked.

I looked at my watch. "I want to schedule the first team meeting for tomorrow morning at 10. Want to come along?"

"I wouldn't miss it," she said, although I got the feeling she was only interested in the entertainment the meeting would surely provide. I would definitely have to find a lot of work for her to do.

What is the Problem?

"Why, that's wonderful, Will!" Jenny told me. She obviously wasn't getting the message.

I tried telling her again. "But my future is riding on this project! And so is Stu's. Remember him? He's my boss. You like him!"

Jenny is my wife. She's a great person, and I value her opinion above just about anyone else's. But she is not terribly sympathetic. She has crazy ideas about dealing with problems in a rational way. Tonight, for example. The whole drive home (which, admittedly, is only about ten minutes since I live on the outskirts of Darfield, the next town over from Enderby) I had been looking forward to complaining about my troubles and then listening to her appropriately sympathetic noises. As usual, she was not playing her part.

"Look, hon," she continued, "from everything you've told me, it seems like Stu made a great decision buying the rights to this product. It should be a great success!"

My wife's positive attitude is something I have always admired. She needs it in her job. Jenny is a freelance journalist. When we had Sarah, our first child, six years ago, Jenny and I decided to move out of the big city (then Baltimore) and live the small town life. We thought it would be better for the kids, and for us. By the time we had our son Jake three years later, I had managed to find the job with Hyler.

Moving to the country sounds like a really trendy thing to do, but we've never regretted it. Unfortunately, Jenny's career was harder hit than mine. Before the kids and the move, she had stories published in *Newsweek* and *Time*. Now, she writes mostly for local papers and magazines.

Anyway, as a writer, Jenny has seen a lot of rejections, often for arbitrary reasons. She has this disgusting habit of shrugging them off and trying again.

I tried once more to convince her it was hopeless. "But, Jen, I don't know anything about construction or installing machinery. And worst of all, I don't know anything about projects!" I could almost feel my lower lip trembling. But my behavior was not inducing the least bit of sympathy.

"Will, it seems to me that you'll be able to get people on your team who have expertise in specific areas. Is that right?"

"I suppose," I admitted grudgingly.

"So your main problem is that you don't know anything about projects."

I hated it when Jenny reduced my nice, big, insurmountable problems to simple, solvable, problems. "It's not that I don't know anything about projects, Jen," I began. "It's just that they always become too big and complicated to handle. It's almost as if the outcome is randomly determined by the Project God, and He is a close relative of Thor."

"Do you honestly believe that a project can't go well?" she asked me.

"I suppose not." I said. "I just haven't run into anyone who knows how to do it." I paused. "Lots of people claim to know. But most of their ideas don't hold up when I try to apply them."

Half a dozen books about projects had made their way across my bedside reading table in the last few years. I had been to three seminars on the topic. All in vain. Sure, I got ideas, but they did not take into account individuals who were disorganized, people who did not want to spend time doing mathematical analysis, or project managers who did not trust their team. Plus, they were always very construction oriented. And most projects I had worked on had a big administrative component that directly affected everything else.

Ironically, while I was able to criticize other people's approaches, I had never figured out an alternative. Whenever I had finished a project, it was time to get on with some other work, or a new project. There was never any time to sit down and learn something from what we had just done. So of course we always did the next project the same way.

"…should go and see Martha." Jenny interrupted my thoughts.

"Sorry, hon, what was that?" I asked.

"I said, if you want to figure out how to do projects better, you should go and see Martha."

I looked at my wife for signs of mental distress. "Martha, your grandmother?" They say that if you want to know what someone will be like in 30 years, just look at his or her parents. I have often wondered if looking at the person's grandparents gives you a picture of what they will be like in 60 years. This always gives me a fright when I think about Jenny's grandmother.

To be fair, the old woman was not that bad. It's just that Martha (as everyone, including her own daughter, calls her) was perhaps the weirdest senior citizen I had ever met. Somewhere in her eighties, she lived with her daughter (Jenny's mother) in Darfield. She apparently spent her time sitting on the porch in her rocking chair, smoking her pipe (yes, a pipe), thinking, and being crusty to people like me. Admittedly, she did have a mind like a steel trap, but she made people uncomfortable (at least people like me), pointing out how someone was doing something wrong, or how they could do it better. The most annoying thing about Martha was that she was almost always right. If she told you there was a better way of doing something, there was. But she would tell you in a way such that you did not want to give her the satisfaction of showing her she was right.

"What does Martha know about projects?" I asked Jenny.

"What do you know about Martha?"

"She's your grandmother, and I often hope your mother was adopted. Other than that, not much. Why?"

Jenny gave me an exasperated look. "If you don't know anything about her, how can you be so sure she can't help you?" There was that logic again.

"I don't approach drunks on the street asking for help on projects, do I?" I asked rhetorically. "And I don't know anything about them either. C'mon, Jenny, you have to give me a reason to go subject myself to her." I liked the way that sounded. You didn't go visit Martha, you subjected yourself to her.

"To be honest, Will, I don't know that much about her background. I do know that when I was a little kid and Martha was living with us, she used to travel all around the country, and even overseas. She would always tell me she was 'helping set people's thinking straight,' as she put it. According to Mom, Martha and my grandfather started a manufacturing business together before the Second World War. They did very well with it, even better after Pearl Harbor. When my grandfather was killed in London in 1942, Martha ran the whole thing herself. I guess she sold out sometime before I was born and came to live with my Mom."

It made sense. Martha seemed like someone who was used to ordering people around. "That's fascinating family history and all, hon, but what makes you think she can help me with launching the WindSailor?" I asked.

"With her experience in business," Jenny answered, "don't you think she might have run across a project or two?"

I sighed. I guessed it wouldn't hurt to talk to her. It probably wouldn't take long. But I had one last line of defense. "Jen, she calls me Willie, and you know how I hate that!"

3

What is a Project?

One thing I've always liked about Darfield is the town's "oldness," the way the whole little village looks like it came from about 1920 (which most of it probably did). The streets are wide and lined with big old elm and oak trees, and behind the trees sit the houses. Big two- and three-story places, with porches that run all the way around the front, houses that really do have the character that real estate listings always claim. Every time I drive through the place, I feel nostalgic for the small town America that was gone before I was born, or perhaps never really existed.

Fortunately my nostalgia is tempered with practicality. Jenny and I were not crazy enough to buy one of those old places—far too much upkeep! When I get home from work I do not want to spend my evenings installing new plumbing, replastering walls, and fixing rotting floor boards.

Jenny's mother and father bought one of the places on Elm Street in the sixties and have been fixing it up ever since. This allows me to live out my big old house dreams whenever I visit, knowing I will soon be returning to a newer place that doesn't require nearly so much work.

Because of this, the prospect of visiting Martha was not all bad.

It was still light out when I pulled into my in-laws' driveway. On this late-August evening the trees were still in full leaf, the air was warm, and you could almost hear kids playing baseball in the vacant lot behind the house.

"Looks like Willie's coming for a visit!" Unfortunately, you could also hear Martha. I got out of the car.

"Hi, Martha," I said politely. She was in her usual place on the porch, sitting in her rocking chair, pipe clenched between her teeth. Sometimes she made me think of a cross-dressing Popeye, but maybe that was being unkind.

Jenny's mother, Natalie, came out through the screen door at the front. "Hi, Will. Jenny called and said you'd be coming over."

"Hi, Natalie," I said. "I just thought I would drop by to visit for a few minutes." I tried to sound casual.

"Would you like some lemonade?" she asked.

"Sure," I said. Lemonade on the front porch on a summer evening. It sure helped my little fantasy along. I walked up the steps and sat in one of the porch chairs close to Martha. "And how are you tonight?" I asked.

"Not too bad, Willie," Martha answered, and then went back to smoking her pipe. I sat there feeling uncomfortable until Natalie brought out my lemonade.

"Here you are, Will," she said, putting it on the small table beside me. "Jenny told me you wanted to talk business with Martha, so I'll just leave you two alone." She turned and went back through the screen door.

We sat in silence for a few more moments while Martha smoked. I have to admit, I love the smell of pipe smoke, regardless of who is producing it.

"Well, Willie," Martha finally said, "you're making me nervous just sitting there. What did you want to talk about?"

I started hesitantly. "Jenny was telling me you used to be a consultant."

"Yes, that's true." she said. "After I quit doing real work I spent some time trying to help other people get their thinking straight."

"Well...," I continued haltingly, "did you ever do any work with projects?"

Martha laughed. Actually, it was more of a guffaw. "Yes, indeed Willie. Why do you want to know?"

I figured what the hell, I'm here. I might as well tell her the story. I gave her a brief overview of my project at Hyler.

"But my real problem isn't really this specific project. It's projects in general. This one is important, but it just points out that I don't know what I'm doing with any project." I felt naked admitting that to Martha. I was worried she would come back with some scathing reply about my lack of intelligence.

Discovering Perspective

To my surprise, that didn't happen. "You've made a big step Willie," Martha said slowly. "I never was able to help straighten out anyone's thinking who didn't understand they had a problem."

I felt absurdly pleased at that comment. "So can you give me some suggestions?" I asked.

Martha looked thoughtful and she took a long draw on her pipe. "You know, Willie, there isn't a lot that I can tell you."

Oh, well, I thought, it's always nice driving down here anyway.

"But what I can do is help *you* figure out how to do projects better." She sat back in her chair looking rather pleased with herself.

I sipped my lemonade. "I don't mean to be rude, Martha, but if I knew what to do, don't you think I would have done it already?"

Martha took her pipe stem from her teeth and said, "Willie," (I'm sure she kept calling me that because she knew it bugged me.) "I bet you already have all the knowledge you need to do projects well."

I reflected on my formal and informal education in project management. I had taken a course in operations research when I was at university. We had done a lot of mathematical analysis of PERT charts and arrow diagrams, both project management tools. But the guy teaching the course had a Ph.D. in project management. It seemed to me there must be a lot of knowledge that I did not yet have. I told this to Martha.

She just smiled. "I suspect that you don't have time to get a Ph.D. before you complete the WindSailor project. And anyway, you probably wouldn't learn much to help you." I had to agree. So far, academic knowledge had been of no help to me in my projects. Martha continued, "If you want to improve the way you do something, like projects, do you always need to increase the quantity of your knowledge?"

"Yes," I said, without hesitation. As soon as the word slipped out, Martha's expression told me I should have thought about it for a little longer. I tried to defend my answer. "Look at all the technological advances we humans have made in the last few years. All the latest discoveries like the silicon chip and fiber optics. They all came from research that increased our knowledge."

"Fiber optics technology has been around since World War II," Martha told me. Like I said, she loves to correct people. "So it hardly qualifies as new technology. However, you are right to a certain extent. New discoveries and solutions do require knowledge, and that knowledge may not yet have been discovered. But I'll ask you again. Is gaining more knowledge always the way to improve things?" She sat back in her chair and tried to take another draw on her pipe. It had gone out by this time, so she busied herself cleaning it out in preparation for re-lighting.

While she was occupied, I thought a little more carefully about the question. Intuitively it made sense that the more you knew, the better you would be able to do things. But I was acquainted with a number of people who seemed to have a large quantity of knowledge but who were not very good at what they did (my project management professor being one of them). I tried to emulate my wife and apply a little logic.

What else would you need except more information to help you improve how you did things? I was beginning to feel impatient. I wanted to spend some time tonight preparing for my morning meeting. I told Martha I was stumped.

"Tell me, Willie," she said. "You're an educated boy. Have you ever heard of Emanuel Kant?"

The line "Emanuel Kant was a real pissant" from a Monty Python song came back to me. That tune was called the "Philosopher's Song," so I took a wild stab. "He was a philosopher, wasn't he?" I asked as nonchalantly as I could manage. It is amazing what you can learn from television.

"Very good," Martha said. "There's hope for you yet. Kant wrote about some interesting things, and one of them relates to our conversation. He made a very important observation about how we humans make new discoveries." She leaned forward in her chair, as if she was getting interested in the conversation. "Kant proposed that the way we choose to look at what we already know is the source of the "new" discoveries that we make. In other words, it is not the acquisition of new information so much as how we look at what we already know that is important in learning new things."

What she was saying appeared to make sense, but I am the kind of person who relates better to examples. "Can you give me an illustration?"

"I'm getting to it," she said, "just let me get my pipe lit." She kept on puffing. One thing I cannot understand about pipe smokers is why it doesn't drive them crazy that their pipe goes out all the time. Come to think of it, maybe they are all crazy. Finally she continued. "The example Kant used is probably one of the best. Did you know that people used to believe that the sun moved around the earth?"

"Yes, and people also used to think the earth was flat."

Martha looked a little annoyed. At least I think she did. It was hard to tell her annoyed looks from her regular ones. "How do you suppose we figured out that the sun didn't go around the earth?"

"I guess somebody made some measurements of the stars or something and worked it out."

"Not at all," Martha said smugly. "Copernicus had exactly the same information that everyone else had at the time. But he also had something else. What do you think it was?"

"I have no idea," I said.

"You don't, but he did," Martha told me. "Copernicus had an idea. That was all. No new knowledge, just an idea. His idea was that maybe the earth revolved around the sun, not the other way around. All the existing knowledge supported that idea, just like it fit into the perspective of the sun going around the earth. But no one had ever thought of it before." Martha sat back smugly in her chair and puffed her pipe. "Kant pointed out that Copernicus had proposed a new mental framework."

I figured she expected me to sum things up like a school boy at the end of the lesson. I summed things up. "So, in order to improve things, or make discoveries about how things are, we might not need new information, just a new perspective on what we already know." The lesson seemed to be ending, and I figured I could be out of there in five minutes.

"That is exactly it, Willie, exactly." She looked as if she had solved all of my problems. Needless to say she had not, especially the one that would occur if Jenny turned into a Martha in the next sixty years.

"So what's your point?" I asked, figuring she didn't have one.

"My point, Willie, is that you don't need to learn a whole lot more about projects. You need to get a new perspective on them."

I stared at her. "Don't keep me in suspense. What's the new perspective?"

"I already told you, I can't tell you what it is. I can only help you discover it for yourself."

This was getting too mystical for me. I stood up. "Well, thanks for your help, Martha," I said, "But I've got to be getting home. I have a big day tomorrow." I started to walk off the porch.

Martha stared over the edge of the railing. She said, "You haven't got it yet, Will." My ears pricked up when she called me that. "But you might. One way or the other, it won't affect me." I stopped on the porch stairs, waiting for her to finish. "I want you to do one thing. Tomorrow, at your team meeting, ask everyone what they mean by the word *project*."

I shook my head and glanced over at the sun sinking into the western horizon. "Good night, Martha," I said as I walked to my car. I figured that Martha was being too theoretical. What could defining projects have to do with anything?

4

The Team Meets

At 9:55 the next morning, I entered the Hyler conference room. There was another meeting still going on. It was a status meeting about a marketing project that was supposed to have ended at 9.

I thought about last night while I waited for the room to clear. When I told Jenny about my conversation with Martha all she said was, "Are you going to ask them?"

"Ask who, what?" I answered.

"Ask your project team what a project is?"

"Hon," I began, "what does that have to do with anything? Everybody knows what a project is!"

Jenny did not want to hear about my troubles after that. All she said was, "Don't write Martha off. She knows what she's doing."

I tried to explain to her that she thought that solely because Martha was a relation, and that there was some kind of trust there because of a complicated Freudian grandmother-granddaughter relationship, but she would have none of it.

By 10:15, everyone was there, and we were ready to start our

10:00 meeting. The team was seated in various places around the conference table. I, of course, occupied the head chair. Interesting, I reflected, how often I had thought that the person sitting in the head chair did not know what he or she was doing. Now I was sitting in that chair, and I knew I had been right.

Gathered around the table were: Amanda Payton, from Information Systems, the infamous Al Burton, from the Industrial and Production Engineering group, his engineering assistant, Sheila Chan, Alice Sorensen, from Accounting, Mark Goldman, from Human Resources, Leslie Frame, from Marketing, and Luigi Delgarno, who was kind of the plant's general foreman.

Except for Al, I was pretty happy with the group. As head of Information Systems, I had worked with all of them on various projects and I had a good relationship with each, including Sheila. I thought she was a better engineer than Al, but that could have been due to that fact that she got along with most people.

I took a deep breath, and then started into my pitch. "As you have all probably heard, Hyler is taking on a new product. We're tentatively calling it WindSailor, and it fits nicely into our product line." I gave them some general information about the product.

"In order to manufacture the WindSailor, we are going to have to make significant changes to our existing plant, including building new space, and buying new equipment. We are also going to hire more people and train them. And we will have to develop some new information systems to support all of this expansion." I took a sip of water. "Our friend, Stu Barnes, the vice-president, is sponsoring this project, and for some reason he has chosen me to manage the whole thing. The only part we will not be responsible for is the marketing campaign. Our Sales and Marketing people will handle that." I stopped for a minute and tried to gauge everyone's reaction to all of this. It appeared more coffee would be needed before I could hope for much response.

"Stu has given me a pretty free rein to run this thing whichever way works. We have to finish everything in time for the production people to make 2,600 boards by June." This produced resentful looks and under the breath mutterings, but at least I was sure the group was alive.

"I am a firm believer in figuring out where we're going before we start spending money," I said, although I was not sure how we were going to do this. "So I want to invest enough up-front planning time to ensure there are no surprises. To facilitate this, I want to run this team in a very informal way. I want everyone involved. If you have ideas, we all want to know about them. If you have criticisms, we want to know about those too." I took a deep breath. "I am not a project management expert. I've worked on a lot of them, but I hardly ever feel I have the control I think I need to do them well. This project is important, expensive, and on a tight deadline. I want to make every effort to ensure it doesn't get away from us." I looked around at all of them. I was hoping this little speech would start pulling us together as a team.

Unfortunately Al spoke first. "I'm not sure what Stu was thinking about, making you project manager. You don't know anything about construction, and that is clearly the most important part of this project." That was Al: the picture of a supportive team player. "It would probably be simpler if you assigned all the construction work to me."

Before I could say anything, Luigi, the general foreman, spoke up. "Al, anytime you do anything around the plant, it screws up operations. When we're not making boats and boards, we're not making money. You don't seem to understand that. Personally, I'm glad you're not in charge of this one. We'd be bankrupt in a week." Al and Luigi exchanged dirty looks.

Alice from accounting piped in. "And I'm sick of running around after you, Al, trying to keep track of your costs and keeping your bills paid. Every time you get involved in something, it creates a big problem for us in Accounting."

They were sounding like the well-functioning team to me. Us against Al. "Regardless of what we all think," I said, "Stu has already decided. Believe me, I tried to convince him he was making a mistake, but he wouldn't buy it." Al stared down at the floor, looking sulky. Everyone else seemed to look pleased, but that was probably my imagination.

"Like I said before, I am no expert on projects. Right now I would like to figure out where we're going and roughly who is going to do what. Where do you guys want to start?"

Trying To Set Goals

"As project manager," Al said, "you should start by establishing the project goals with the team." One thing about Al you had to admire: personal animosity from everyone he worked with would not stop him from speaking what he thought was the truth.

"Okay, Al," I said, "let's begin with project goals." I got up and walked to the flip chart. "I'll write them up as we go."

Leslie volunteered the first one. "I think the main goal of your project, as well as the Marketing project, is to make the WindSailor a big success for Hyler."

That sounded good to me, and everyone nodded agreement. On the flip chart I wrote:

Project Goal: Make the WindSailor a success

Sheila, Al's assistant, had some concerns with that. She said, "That sounds pretty fuzzy. If we are going to make that the goal, should we have some kind of measurement of success?"

Leslie said, "How about meeting the projected sales of 2,600 units in the first year?"

Under the first line on the flip chart, I wrote:

by meeting the first season sales target of 2,600 units.

"Everyone happy with that?" I asked.

Luigi said, "How about putting something in about minimizing disruption to our current production operation, which, I will remind you all, is what gives us grocery money every week."

I hesitated with the pen. "I'm not sure how that would be classified. It's not really a goal…"

Al said, "In project management terms, that would be a sub-goal. See, it supports the main goal, but it's secondary."

I still hesitated. I was starting to wonder exactly how goals and sub-goals, and maybe even sub-sub-goals, were going to help us.

Al looked a little peeved that I had not written down his suggestion. "For God's sakes, Will, I'm a certified project manager. I know about goals and sub-goals. It's the accepted way to do it."

Certified people always made me nervous, but I wrote on the flip chart:

Project Sub-Goal 1:
To conduct the project in such a way as to minimize the negative impact on our existing production operation.

Alice said, "If we are going to include this kind of stuff, I want something in there about doing this project so it doesn't cause me and my staff another million accounting headaches."

"Fair enough," I said. On the flip chart I wrote:

Project Sub-Goal 2:
To conduct the project in such a way as to minimize conflict with the accounting function.

I turned to Alice for approval. "How's that?"

"Fine," she said. "If you can get anyone to pay attention to it."

Al chimed in with his comments on accounting. "Look Alice, the reason I don't bother getting anything to you on time is that your costing system doesn't work for projects." I hated to admit it, but I agreed with Al. Fortunately, Sheila spoke up and saved me the trouble of doing so publicly.

"He's right you know," Sheila said. "Any reports you provide us are always so far out of date they're useless."

Alice looked a little flustered. "Look," she said defensively, "my main responsibility is to keep track of financial information for the company. All this project stuff is just a sideline for me. I don't have the resources to be able to jump every time you people want something!"

I sensed more of a problem, so I stepped in. "Obviously getting enough resources will be important. Everyone, including Alice, will have to let me know what your requirements are well in advance. With Stu's help we should be able to hire extra staff, or whatever it takes, to get this work done." Personally, I hoped that we could figure out very soon what kind of resources we would need. "Let's get back on track. Any other goals or sub-goals we need to add?"

"What about the budget?" Leslie asked.

"Good point," I said. "Our budget on this one, as officially approved by the Hyler Board, is $1 million."

"That's a nice round number," Amanda said. "From outer space."

Al must have agreed with her. "It really doesn't help to put the budget or the schedule in the statement of project goals. It will just get you into trouble. The cost and schedule change all the time anyway, and changes upset the sponsor."

"Are you nuts?" Mark Goldman, the Human Resources guy, asked. "Don't you think Stu is going to want to know that we're at least aware of when this is supposed to finish and how much it will cost?"

Al leaned back and assumed his most annoying I-know-what-I'm-talking-about-and-you-know-nothing look. "We don't want to get hung out to dry when we can't meet some unrealistic budget and schedule put together by some turkey who doesn't know anything about the project. Let's just put in a sub-goal about doing all of this work on time and on budget, but let's not write down what the time and budget are. It will save us a lot of headaches in the long run."

I wasn't sure what to do with this one. Most of the projects I had worked on had some time frame and cost that was pulled out of thin air. Invariably, by the time the thing was done, one or both were significantly different from when I started.

"Al, what does the sponsor say when you leave those two things out of project goals?"

Al looked a bit sheepish. "To be honest, I've never been able to get a sponsor to go for that." Everyone let out an exasperated sigh. "But it's a good idea!" he said quickly. "If you can get it by the sponsor."

I did not like the idea of trying to "get anything by" the sponsor. We were supposed to be working together, but past experience had me in agreement with Al. On the flip chart I wrote:

Project Sub-Goal 3:
To conduct the project in such a way as to complete it on time
and within the specified budget.

As I finished writing, Mark said, "I'll tell you right now, that looks stupid. I for one vote to put the schedule and budget constraints up there before we go any further."

I turned to the group. "What do the rest of you think?" There were various murmurings for and against the idea of including the cost. The only thing that I could determine was that there was no agreement.

I decided to move on. "Maybe we can agree after thinking about it for a while." I turned back to the flip chart. "Anybody have anything to add?" No one did. "Right," I said. "Moving along. We've identified the project goals. What about responsibilities?"

As usual, Al had some suggestions. "Let's just divide things up functionally. I'll handle all the construction and equipment stuff, Mark will handle personnel, Alice, accounting, and so on."

"So what do I do?" I asked. This did not sound like teamwork.

"You coordinate." Al said.

Before I could respond, Amanda spoke up. "Al, you know that isn't going to work. There's too much interaction among all the areas."

"Look," Al said. "If each person looks out for themselves, we will be able to work efficiently. When I need something from one of you, I'll let you know. If you can't supply it, I'll take care of it myself. And we track our own costs."

Alice's face turned very red. "When you do that, you make my job even more difficult! You don't tell me what you're spending where, and then I have to deal with suppliers who want to know why I haven't paid them!" Alice sat back and crossed her arms. "If I had a choice, I wouldn't even be here."

Then Mark added fuel to the fire. "You have to admit, Alice, that things do run on a different schedule in accounting."

Alice blew up again. "That's because no one ever tells us anything! We only find out what's going on when you guys start to complain!"

I suppose that I should have been happy. My team was starting to spread the blame already, a skill we would likely need in the coming months.

Al said, "If we would just divide up the responsibilities, each of us could figure out the work to be done on our own, and we wouldn't have to waste anymore time in this meeting."

"I agree with Al," Leslie said. "Let's just figure out what we each need to do and get on with it."

Amanda jumped in. "I already explained to you, Leslie, everything we do is going to have some impact on everyone else."

I tossed the marker on the table and sat down. My mind drifted out of the conversation as everyone started talking at once. I thought, at least this meeting is not like any other project team meeting I have been involved in: it's worse. What we had achieved so far was a very fuzzy project goal, a couple of fuzzy sub-goals that would apply to any project being done at Hyler (or anywhere else), and a lot of disagreement about how to do things.

I tried to get a little perspective on why things were going as poorly as they were. Granted, people from different functional areas were bound to have their own ideas about projects and what was important. But a project in accounting would follow the same basic process as a project in marketing or construction, although the end product would be different. Or would they really be the same? And what if everyone thought they were different? Perception is reality, as they say. If a bunch of people have a different understanding about a situation, might it not be hard to get consensus on how to proceed? And suppose that not only did everyone have a different understanding, but everyone's understanding was wrong. Not completely wrong, but maybe off just a bit.

A Variety of Answers

I went to the flip chart and turned over a fresh page. "What is a project?" I asked the group.

No one responded because they were all busy arguing. They started to quiet down when they saw me standing there.

"What was your question, Will?" Amanda asked.

"What is a project?" I repeated. "What is the definition of a project?"

"No offense, Will, but what does this have to do with anything?" Mark asked.

"Look," I said, "I think this will help. What is a project?"

"It's some work that has a goal," Amanda volunteered.

I nodded and wrote that on the flip chart. "That's not exactly it," said Mark. "It also has a beginning and an end and a lifecycle," I added that to the chart.

"It has a budget and a schedule," said Alice.

"It has resources assigned," added Leslie.

"It's a one-time activity," Luigi said. "You never do it again. It's unique."

"It's a bunch of tasks that achieve a goal," Mark said.

I frantically scribbled all of this on the flip chart.

Then Al said: "A project is any undertaking which has a defined start and end point and which sets specific objectives to be accomplished. Projects are unique, time-limited, goal-oriented, major undertakings, and require a commitment of varied skills and resources." Without even pausing for breath he continued, "Project management is the discipline that has developed a set of tools, methodologies, and a process to manage projects. Specifically, project management is the art of directing and coordinating human and material resources throughout the life of a project, by using modern management techniques to achieve pre-determined objectives of scope, quality, time, cost, and participant satisfaction."

It sounded like something he had memorized from a text book. I tried to jot down a few of the highlights. "Anyone have anything else?"

"That's a nice definition and all," Amanda said to Al, "but if that's a project, what isn't?" She was right. Al's definition could be applied to just about anything.

Al apparently agreed. "If you choose," said Al, "you can manage anything as a project."

I felt confused. Everything could be managed as a project? It was time to move on. I stepped back and looked at what I had written on the flip chart. "Anybody notice anything about all of these definitions?" I asked.

"Yeah," said Luigi. "You killed a lot of trees to write them all down. Where is this going?" No one else said anything.

The problem was, I didn't know where this was going. I just knew there was something important here that I didn't want to miss.

"Nowhere," I answered. "It's almost 11. I would like each of you to make a list of the things that need to be done in your area, or with your area, and one of the others. Have that done by tomorrow, and we will meet at 1 p.m. Then we'll try to put the lists together and come up with some kind of integrated plan."

Grumbling, everyone got up and left the conference room. I didn't blame them for feeling dissatisfied; I felt that way myself. I went to the flip chart and tore off the pages we had used. When I turned around, Al was the only person still in the room.

"Will," he began, "quite frankly, I don't think you have the knowledge or the experience to do a good job on this. Ralph Borsellino thinks along the same lines. He wants me to make sure that you stick to the rules on this one so it doesn't get away from you." He paused and looked at his notes. "So think of me as the policeman on the team. I'll be looking for things you're doing wrong, and I'll be letting Ralph know. But I'll also be telling you what I tell Ralph, so don't think I will be trying to stab you in the back." I didn't feel comforted, but at least he was honest. "I'm just hoping you will screw up early enough that I can save the project when they turn it over to me."

On second thought, there was such a thing as too much honesty.

"Now," he said, "as I understand it, Ralph wants a work breakdown structure. You haven't mentioned that to the team yet. He also wants to see earned value costing reports. You haven't told Alice about that yet." He studied his notes. "And," he continued, "you haven't told them about integrating this with the TQM project."

Another two items, and physical violence would have been unavoidable. "Listen, Al," I said with controlled anger, "I expect you to bring these things up with the entire group. I don't need you giving me a private report card when everyone has left the room." I paused. "And anyway, what does Ralph want that stuff for? He probably doesn't even know what a work breakdown structure is."

"He wants that stuff, as you call it, because I told him he wants it! He doesn't have to understand why." Al glared at me as he put his notes away. "It's not easy being the project manager. Just remember, I'll be watching." He picked up his briefcase and walked out of the room.

I slumped into one of the chairs and stared at the ceiling. I was doubly disadvantaged. Not only was I not a project expert, but I hated office politics, and it seemed that Al was intent on playing them to make me look bad. Neither he nor Ralph seemed to realize that making me look bad could have serious consequences for this project, and for Hyler.

5

Sifting Through the Mess

Back at my office, I sat down in my chair and put my feet up on my desk. Although people have told me that this particular position looks arrogant, disrespectful, lazy, and just plain impolite, I find it to be extremely comfortable. Whenever I need to think, I always sit like this and stare at the ceiling, sort of my own version of Rodin's sculpture.

I spent a moment examining my motives. I had worked on many projects before this one without spending so much time wondering if there was a better way. Why now? Was it the size? Was it my unfamiliarity with so many aspects of the project? Maybe because my career with this company was riding on it? Anyway, it didn't matter why. I would just have to continue trying to figure out a better way.

That decided, I stuck the flip charts from the meeting around the walls of my office. I looked first at the project goals. It read:

Project Goal:
Make the WindSailor a success by meeting the first
season sales target of 2,600 units.

Project Sub-Goal 1:
To conduct the project in such a way as to minimize the negative
impact on our existing production operation.

Project Sub-Goal 2:
To conduct the project in such a way as to minimize
conflict with the accounting function.

Project Sub-Goal 3:
To conduct the project in such a way as to complete it
on time and within the specified budget.

I felt uneasy with them. It wasn't that I disagreed with any of them, it was just that they didn't seem to provide me with anything that would help me do the project better. Maybe they were not specific enough.

I gave up on the goals and looked at the definitions of the word *project*. Like I thought before, they were all a little different, and all a little vague. Take the one that went: "Something with a beginning and an end and a lifecycle." Sure, this was a characteristic of a project, but a phrase like that could be talking about a giraffe, and I was not prepared to admit that giraffes were projects. So what was the definition of the word project? Suddenly, I had an idea. Where do you go when you want to know the definition of a word? Of course! The dictionary.

I hustled down to the file room and helped myself to the big fat *Oxford Concise Dictionary* and returned to my office.

Feet up on the desk again, I began flipping through the pages looking for the word project. I always have a little trouble finding words in dictionaries. Maybe I didn't learn my alphabet properly as a kid. In fact, my wife always teases me about it. As a result, I always open the book up well before the word I am looking for, just so I don't miss it. As I turned pages toward the p's, a couple of words caught my eye: *fetal*—the position I felt like curling up in right about then, *hateful*—which described my feelings towards Al, *Pizarro*— Spanish conqueror of Peru—you never know when this might come up in Trivial Pursuit. Finally, I found the word project. It said:

> project (noun): plan, scheme, planned undertaking

I copied this definition onto one of the flip chart sheets. Then I sat down again, put my feet up, and stared at the words. A project is a plan. That is it? The word *plan* was not in any of the definitions I had heard from my project team. Even Al's long, rambling one did not say anything about a plan.

I tried to consider things logically. What did a plan have to do with a project? Intuitively, one would think it obvious that a plan is required for a project. So how come no one mentioned it? I knew from experience that most projects do not have anything that one might call a plan. Actually, that was not quite true. Someone always claimed to have a plan inside their head, but I could never be sure because I could not see in there.

This line of thought prompted the question: why make a plan? We make a plan, I decided, to help us organize all of our jumbled ideas about how we want things to go in the future, and what we are going to do to make things turn out that way.

I got up and went to the flip chart again. Underneath the dictionary definition of the word *project* I wrote:

> A plan helps us structure our thoughts about:
> - How we want the future to be.
> - What we have to do to make that future happen.

I felt I was onto something. Just then the phone rang.

"So how did the first meeting go?" It was Stu.

"Not too badly," I lied. "There seems to be a little disagreement about how to proceed, but we'll get around it."

"That's good," said Stu, "because there's going to be a meeting of the Hyler board of directors tomorrow evening at the Four Seasons Hotel in Portland."

I was a little surprised. "You mean a face-to-face meeting?" Hyler's board included several key executives from Mantec. They were busy people, and most Hyler board meetings were held via conference call.

"Yeah," Stu confirmed. "They want to meet with Ralph and make sure this WindSailor project is going to go okay."

"So I guess you'll have to give them a little presentation on the project?" I asked, thinking of all the information he was probably going to want before tomorrow night.

"Actually," said Stu, "you are going to do the presentation."

"Why me? It was your idea!"

Stu chuckled. "Both Ralph and I thought the board might be interested in hearing from you directly, instead of from those of us who are a little removed from the whole thing."

My heart sank. "What are they going to want to see?"

"That's up to you," Stu said. "I just want you to show them that we're in control of this thing."

"It hasn't even started yet!" I moaned. "I haven't had time to do much of anything with it."

"Talk to me tomorrow afternoon so you can give me a run-through of what you're going to tell them." He hung up.

My first impulse was to start throwing task lists, charts, graphs, cost estimates, and coffee beans together for the presentation. Fortunately, my innate sense of sloth prevailed. I decided to spend at least a little more time on what I had been thinking about before Stu called. I looked at what I had just written about why we plan. Of course! A plan does serve to structure our thinking about where we want to go and how we will get there, but just as importantly, *it serves as a communication device!* And not only is a plan a communication device to other people, it also serves to remind you of what your intentions were. No wonder I used to question people who said they had the plan all thought out in their heads. There was no way they could communicate it! Just thinking about something does not mean you have planned it. You still need to be able to communicate it.

Before I could forget, I jumped up and wrote on the flip chart:

A plan:
- Helps structure your thinking.
- Communicates your intentions.

I didn't know why, but I felt like this was important.

I forwarded my phone, grabbed my jacket, and headed out the door. It was only 11:30, but I had more important places to be. It was time to visit Martha again.

6

Asking the Right Questions

I didn't take the time to notice the big houses and the tree-lined streets on this drive through Darfield. I was too busy thinking about projects, plans, and presentations. Wherever I was going with all of this, I hoped that I could get there in a big hurry.

As I swung into my in-laws' driveway I could see Martha sitting on the porch in her rocking chair, smoking her pipe, just as I left her the night before. She was reading and looked up as I got out of the car. "Aren't you supposed to be at work, Willie?"

"A project is a plan!" I said as I rushed up onto the porch and sat down in the chair beside her.

She smiled a little and took the pipe out of her mouth. "I'm surprised to see you back here, Willie," she said. "Seems to me I wasn't giving you much help last night."

"I got to thinking about the question you asked when I was leaving," I admitted. "I pretty much forgot about it until things started to fall apart as usual at the first project meeting today. When I asked the group your question, everyone gave me a different answer.

I looked up the word *project* in the dictionary and, well, things started to make more sense. And since it was your idea, I decided I needed to come talk to you again."

Just then the front door opened and my father-in-law, Fred, walked out. Fred works the afternoon shift at the local sawmill, so he is usually home until about three. "Oh, hello, Will," he said. "Aren't you supposed to be at work?" It seemed like a popular question, and I started to feel like I was 17 and cutting school.

"I had to talk some things over with Martha," I explained. "I won't be long."

"Nat!" Fred yelled back into the house. "Will is here, and he'll be staying for lunch!" I started to refuse, but Fred would have none of it.

"So," Martha said as Fred went out to the garage, "you've figured out that a project has something to do with a plan. Did you think about what a plan is good for?"

Feeling absurdly pleased, I said, "A plan has two purposes: it helps structure your thinking, and it allows you to communicate your intentions."

"Very good." Martha sounded surprised. "So what did you come out here to ask me?" Her pipe was out, and she pulled her tobacco pouch out of her dress, and started stuffing tobacco into it (the pipe, not her dress).

That one stumped me for a second. Why had I come rushing out here? "To be honest, Martha, I'm not really sure. You got me thinking about what a project really is, and about what a plan is good for. How can we do a project if we don't even agree on what it is? And if a plan is for communicating, how do we record the decisions and logic that make up a plan." I paused. "The thing is, I have to make a presentation to the Hyler board of directors tomorrow about this project, and I don't think they're going to be impressed with what I've got so far. I need you to help me figure out what all this means, and take me to the next step."

By now, Martha had her pipe going again, and she eyed me speculatively. "You didn't seem all that keen last night." She sort of sighed this out and then stared into the distance, playing the injured party.

I figured a full apology was in order. "Martha, I'm sorry I doubted your approach, but I'm ready to listen now."

She turned and looked at me. "I can help you figure things out, but if I tell you things, you won't understand the why, and you won't be able to use the ideas properly. Then you'll blame me when things go wrong." I didn't bother to disagree.

Martha leaned forward in her chair. "Ignorance ain't so much not knowin', as knowin' a lot of stuff that ain't so. You ever hear that, Will?" I shook my head. "Will Rogers said that a long time ago and it is still true today. And it doesn't just apply to projects!" She was really getting going now. "You see, people always want things to be better, but they never want to change how they do things. If you want to do projects better, you're going to have to change how you do them."

"So, what do I do differently?"

"Remember what we talked about last night?" she asked. "About mental frameworks? That's what you are going to have to change if you want to improve projects."

I was game to try. "Okay. Where do we start?"

"You tell me," Martha said.

I was ready for this one. "Well, I understand the purpose of a plan, and I understand that we need a plan to have a project, but it seems to me that there are all sorts of things in a project that just aren't covered by that simple definition of project."

"A good place to start," Martha said. "Fetch me a piece of paper." I went back to my car and got a pad from the passenger seat.

Martha took the pad and right in the middle wrote the word *project*. She asked me, "What was the definition of this word again?"

I told her, "Plan, or planned undertaking."

"So which is it?" she asked.

"Which is what?" I answered.

"Which is the definition of project? We need to clarify what we mean by the word project if we are going to be able to think about it in a useful way." She looked at me.

Was a project a plan, or was it the undertaking, the one the plan was for? It was like saying: is a project the cake or the recipe for making the cake? "I'm not sure," I said with finality.

Martha gave a little disgusted sigh. "The dictionary won't solve all your problems. You still have to think. Is it more useful to think of a project as a plan, or as the thing that the plan is about?"

"A project is a plan," I said finally. "It makes more sense to think about the finished product as whatever it is, and reserve the word project for how you are going to get the finished product."

Martha seemed please by this. "Good idea. But if a project is a plan, are all plans necessarily projects?"

This women was driving me nuts with her questions. I thought about the classic false syllogism. All dogs have feet. All rats have feet. All rats are dogs.

I considered plans. There were strategic plans, project plans, house plans, game plans, and God knew what other types of plans. So the question was: Is a strategic plan the same as a project plan? I didn't think so.

"I guess all plans are not necessarily projects," I said.

"Which means," continued Martha, "that a project is a special type of plan. In fact, a project is a special type of plan called an execution plan."

On the pad of paper she wrote:

project = execution plan

"It sounds to me like the execution plan just describes the actual work to produce the final product." I said.

"Exactly," said Martha.

"So," I continued, "if you were building a house, the execution plan would just be the plan for pouring the foundations, putting up the walls, painting, and all of that. Is that right?"

"Exactly," Martha repeated.

I had a problem with this. "There has to be more to it than that! What about project initiation, and the design? What about where you figure out if you want a three bedroom house or a one bedroom? That doesn't fit anywhere in this definition."

Martha stopped rocking and leaned forward. "That is exactly right." I got the feeling that there was an important message here.

Martha leaned back and started sucking on her pipe again. It was out, which was how it seemed to spend most of its existence, so I had a chance to ponder while she re-filled.

If the definition of a project did not include all of that other stuff, it didn't mean the other stuff didn't get done. "Martha," I said, "you're telling me that project initiation and design, and even the actual execution, are not part of the project."

She nodded. "I didn't say they weren't part of the project manager's job, I just said they weren't part of the project." Her pipe was going again and she took a few puffs. "Think about a golf game, Willie. It really helps your game if you use the right club. Now what helps you determine which club to use?"

The answer was obvious. "Where the ball lies," I said.

"That's right. If you're driving off the tee, you might select your three-wood or your driver. If you're in a sand trap, you might choose a wedge, and if you're on the green, you would likely select a putter."

"Now suppose for a minute that you're a really great putter." That was a hard supposition for me to make, but I let her proceed. "You can sink anything within 25 feet of the hole. Let's also suppose that your driving isn't all that great. You have a bad slice, and most of the time when you hit off the tee, you end up in the next fairway or in the bushes. But once you get on the green, you're very accurate. Would you consider using your putter to hit off the tee since you have so much success with that club?"

"Of course not," I answered.

"Why not?" she countered.

"Well...because it's the wrong club. It would take a lot of putts to get you anywhere near the green. Your best bet would be to try and improve your driving."

Martha puffed out a thick cloud of smoke. "I want to point out a couple of things to you." She gestured with her index finger. "First, things we would not think of doing in a golf game we do all the time in real life. When we find that something is successful, we tend to apply it to the same thing over and over again, even though the situation has changed. How much sense does that make?"

"Second,"—she gestured with her middle finger—"to know what tool, or club, you should apply to help you out, you need to look around. You can't make a good decision about any club until you know where you are on the course. So with projects, the first things we need to understand are: what does the course look like, and where are we? We need to know that so we can figure out the best club, or tool, to apply to get us closer to the hole. It doesn't guarantee success, but it certainly increases our chances."

Martha stared hard at her pipe. It had gone out during this little speech and she started the re-lighting process once more. All that fiddling with lighting and re-lighting would drive me crazy if I were a pipe smoker.

"I think I am a little short in the club department," I said.

"It isn't the only place, Willie," Martha said brightly, "but don't worry. There's another way projects are like golf. You can acquire a huge bag of clubs, but you only need a few basic ones to play the game."

Just then my mother-in-law stuck her head out of the screen door. "You folks ready for some lunch?" Natalie asked.

"Sure am!" Martha answered before I could say anything. "Willie is tiring me out. Don't worry," she said to me when she saw the look on my face, "we'll talk more after we eat."

It was a summer style lunch of cucumber and tomato sandwiches and it was quite refreshing to stop thinking hard for a few moments and talk about the weather and other important things with my in-laws. By the time everyone had finished eating, I was ready to get back to work.

"I know you two have a lot to talk about," said Natalie as she got up from the table. "You go on back outside and I'll clean up."

Normally I am quite diligent about not leaving someone else to do all the cleanup work, but this time I was happy to oblige. Martha was already in her chair, working on her pipe, when I returned to the porch. That pipe seemed to play a major part in her life, so I asked Martha about it.

"This old thing? Why Donald used to smoke a pipe, and I always loved the smell. After he died, I just couldn't bear to live without it, so I took it up myself. It always reminds me of him." She stared into the middle distance thinking, I assumed, of Donald.

We sat in silence for a few minutes as I waited for Martha to begin again. Finally, I decided to take the initiative.

"So, Martha, can you help me see the layout of the course?" I figured staying with her analogy might be a good idea.

"As you know, Willie, every golf course is different, just like every project, and the things that surround it are different. But just as there are elements common to every golf course, there are some fundamental principles that describe what goes on around a project. In order to be successful, we must understand these."

Martha took the pad of paper and pencil and wrote:

> GENESIS
> DESIGN
> EXECUTION PLAN (PROJECT)
> EXECUTION
> REVIEWS (3)

I looked at it for a moment. It was not talking, so I looked at Martha. "And?" I prompted.

"All projects have the same structure, Willie, and these words describe that structure. Once you understand the structure, you can apply the right tools and get the job done." She looked proud of herself, as if these words represented a lot of work for her.

I looked again at the paper. It seemed to represent most of what I would have said a project was. I noticed, though, that the word project didn't show up until halfway down, beside "Execution Plan."

"Why don't you just call this whole thing a project?"

Martha lowered her eyebrows and a dark cloud seemed to pass over her face. In fact, until she lowered them, I never realized how dark her eyebrows really were. "Did you forget what we talked about before lunch? You told me a project was a plan."

"Well," I said defensively, "isn't this whole thing on your paper a plan?"

"This," said Martha, "is a framework that describes what happens around projects. Clearly, we need to have more discussion about planning in general."

I felt desperate. "Martha, I'm afraid I just don't have time for that. I'll take your word for it: this is a framework, not a project. Let's just go from there."

I could tell that she did not really want to, but in the end my pleading look won out. "Okay," she said, "but it's a discussion we need to have later. In order to be clear, you must accept that a project is a special type of plan called an execution plan."

"Fine," I said, "but what do I call all this stuff that includes a project?"

Martha drew on her pipe before she answered. "There is no really good name for it, but I call it an Assignment." She circled all the words and wrote Assignment beside them.

"Good," I said, "I'll call it an Assignment. Now explain genesis. What goes on during that phase?"

"Willie, think about each one of these phases in terms of what should result from its completion. Knowing what must come out of it will determine what should be going on during the particular phase."

That made a lot of sense. Let the end determine the means. "Fine," I said. "So what is the result of genesis?"

Martha just looked at me and smoked her pipe. Then I remembered; she was going to help me figure it out, she was not going to just tell me. I sat back in my chair. How did most projects—excuse me *assignments*—begin? Usually some higher-up in the organization decided he or she wanted to make an impact, so they would set something in motion, hopefully for the better.

"Genesis is when someone in a company decides to change things," I said.

"That's part of what is going on, but what is the result?"

The result was usually some executive's rough ideas about what should be done. Half the problems with assignments seemed to be that the executive in question was not really sure what he or she wanted.

"The result of genesis would be some kind of fuzzy statement about what was supposed to be done."

"Even with your editorial slant, you are pretty much correct." She wrote on the pad of paper:

> Genesis (Results):
> An idea about how to improve the existing situation

It sounded airy-fairy at first, but the more I thought about it, the more I realized that was exactly how projects started. They did not always improve things, but that was their intent. Something was missing though. "Shouldn't there be something in there about the project sponsor or champion, the person who's idea it was?"

"You're partly right, Willie," Martha told me, "although you have made an assumption that is not always true. Do the ideas for assignments always originate high in the organization, with people who are likely to be sponsors?"

I was a little confused. In our company, lower level people often got assigned to be project sponsors, but the ideas for the projects always got approved by people higher up.

Then I realized what I was assuming. Ideas *could* come from anywhere, but they needed to be approved by someone who had authority.

"So not only does there need to be the idea," I told Martha, "there also needs to be some kind of authority behind it."

On the paper, Martha added:

> Genesis (Results):
> An idea about how to improve the existing situation.
> An assignment of the authority to act.

"What else?" I asked, eager to hear more.

"What else what?" Martha replied.

"What else is there that is supposed to come out of genesis? There must be more. People need more than this when they do multimillion-dollar projects. What about project goals and sub-goals and work breakdown structures and all of that?"

"Willie, my boy, the beauty of letting the results you require determine your actions is that you waste little effort on superfluous things." She looked at the floor and said in a distracted way, "Assuming of course you pick the right results." She looked up at me again. "But never mind about that. Getting that clear definition is the first phase in an Assignment. Once we have completed that, we have the results we need to go on to the design phase. That's the beauty of this framework. Each successive phase depends on the previous one. You know you did the last one right if you can do the next one."

"If that's true," I asked, "how come I've never seen this framework?"

Martha just looked at me and did not say anything for a moment. "Seems to me," she said then, "that I've heard of more than a few 'projects' not going too well." That was certainly true. You couldn't open up a newspaper without reading about some mega-project that was four years late and $800 million over budget. "And besides," Martha said, "people do follow this to some extent because this framework deals with how projects actually happen. However, most people working on projects have their heads down and when one or more of the phases is not completed properly, it leads to all sorts of troubles. You'll see what I mean as we go, Willie." Her nickname for me was really starting to grate.

"Okay, Martha, I know what the result of genesis should be. Any suggestions on how to get that clear description of the idea about how to improve the situation?"

"As a matter of fact, I do." Martha wrote eight questions on the paper. They were:

1. What is wrong with the existing situation?
2. How will things be better when we are done?
3. What are the performance criteria? (How does this thing have to perform when it is completed?)
4. What is the scope of the Assignment? (What is in and what is out?)
5. What are the other constraints (cost, time, quality)?
6. Who is the Sponsor?
7. Who is the Project Manager?
8. What authority is being given?

She handed me the paper. "I call the answers to these questions the Objective Statement. And I think we are just about finished for the day."

"Finished?" I asked, "but I haven't even answered these questions." I felt panicked.

"Willie, I can't answer the questions. I need to have a rest." She didn't look tired to me. I gave her my wounded-dog look. I may even have whimpered.

"She frowned and then said, "Okay, here's a couple more things. You need to be able to identify the sponsor and the project manager. What is the one characteristic that tells you who the sponsor is?"

"Authority," I said. "The sponsor usually has some authority over the project."

"Close," said Martha. "What gives the sponsor that authority?"

I thought for a second. "Money! The sponsor controls the cash."

"Correct," Martha said. "The sponsor controls the money. You have to know who is making the money decisions, because that person has ultimate control over the entire assignment. He or she is the person you must go to when changes happen because the sponsor is your client and he or she is paying the bills."

"Another thing," Martha continued, "You must get the objective statement signed. By whom and why?"

I felt like I was on Jeopardy, saying, "Projects for $600, Alex." Instead, I said, "The sponsor should sign off the objective statement. As to why, I suppose because that way I, as the project manager, can cover my butt if the sponsor starts to change his mind." I knew the signing thing would not go over well at Hyler.

Martha sighed. "The signature is a cultural ritual. It indicates the sponsor has read, understood, and agreed to the objective statement. It is not supposed to be used for assigning blame. It shows the project manager that the person who will be paying the bills is clear on what he or she wants. If the custom was to cut the heads off chickens and wave them in the air while dancing naked around a bonfire, then I'd tell you to do that. The signature is a mechanism that gets the sponsor on board. Without it, you are at the mercy of the whimsical sponsor. And remember, the objective statement will change."

Great, I thought. We'll put all this work into something just so we can change it.

Martha went on, "At the start, we really know very little about the assignment. It is just someone's idea about how to make the world a better place. As we get further into it, we will learn more and more, and that may change our original assumptions about how the assignment was going to be. Whenever that happens, *you must update the objective statement*!" She punctuated each syllable in the last few words by tapping the pencil on the armrest of her rocker. "And you must get the sponsor to sign each new objective statement. Otherwise, the sponsor will be out of date, and probably not happy to learn about the changes."

I was frantically making notes as she told me all of this. When I finished writing, I said, "It seems like a lot of work."

Martha lowered her eyebrows again. "Shouldn't you be meeting with your project team right now?"

I took the hint.

7

Writing the Objective Statement

As I drove back to the office, the excitement of Martha's revelations started to fade. I still was not convinced that they were taking me anywhere that was going to make Stu or Ralph happy. Nevertheless, I was determined to change things, so I resolved to stick with Martha's ideas.

When I got in, a stack of pink message slips sat on my desk, and my in-basket was full of memos, notes, letters, and other urgent things. Fortunately, I can ignore the urgent in favor of the really, really urgent.

Twenty minutes later my project team was sitting around a big table in the Dunkin' Donuts shop across the street from the plant. The conference room had been booked and no one had an office big enough for the eight of us.

The faces around the table were not looking pleased despite the fact that I had sprung for a 24 pack of donut holes. It sat untouched in the center of the table.

Mark spoke first. "What is this about, Will? We all have a lot of work to do, and I for one haven't had a chance to put anything together on this project yet."

I wasted no time. "Like I told all of you this morning, I want to do whatever it takes to get control of this project. I wasn't all that pleased with what we achieved at our meeting, so I contacted an outside consultant for some assistance." I had decided to exaggerate a little with respect to Martha. I figured if I didn't, none of these new ideas would have credibility with my team.

No one except Al seemed interested in the news. I suspected he was a little ticked off that I would go outside instead of coming to him. I continued, "The consultant introduced me to a framework that describes what happens during a project."

For the next 15 minutes, I gave them a condensed version of my discovery in the dictionary, the purpose of a plan, and my conversation with Martha, concluding with the fact that we were at the genesis stage in this particular assignment.

When I was done, Alice asked, "So we don't even use the word project right?"

"It's not really about right and wrong," I told her. "The point is that if we agree on what we mean by the words, we have a solid foundation. If we don't agree, we'll be flailing around in the dark."

Heads around the table were starting to nod and Luigi said, "It would be nice if we were all thinking about things the same way for once."

Al did not agree. "This is a waste of time! I've already told you what a project is, and this doesn't have anything to do with it." He stood up and looked at me. "I'll be talking to Ralph." With that, he pushed his chair back into the table and left.

Everybody was silent for a few minutes. Finally Leslie said, "If Al doesn't like these ideas, well, that says something for them." This made everyone smile.

"So what does your consultant say is the next step?" asked Mark.

I pulled out the sheet with Martha's questions written on it. "We need to clearly define what the assignment is," I said, "and to do that, we need to produce an objective statement."

"That should be easy," said Amanda, "since we've already got our project goals."

"The project goals will probably help us, but we need to answer each question pretty specifically."

"So, what are the questions?" Amanda asked.

I read the first one aloud. "What is wrong with the existing situation?"

Everyone looked at each other. "Nothing," said Leslie. "Everything is fine."

We all thought about that for a second, and then Amanda said, "But the result of genesis is supposed to be an idea about how to improve the situation."

"That doesn't mean there's anything wrong," retorted Leslie. "It just means there is an idea about how to make things even better."

"But if there isn't anything wrong," said Amanda, "then how can we make things even better, as you say?"

Fortunately, Sheila came to our rescue. "Look you guys, you're getting emotional about the words instead of thinking about what they really mean. It's obvious what's wrong with the existing situation. There is an opportunity to exploit—the new product—and Hyler doesn't have the facilities to take advantage of it."

As I looked around the table, people's heads started nodding again. "When you put it that way, Sheila, it seems pretty obvious," Mark said. "What is wrong is we can't take advantage of the opportunity. I like it."

"Let's not get too happy about everything yet," I interrupted. "Who volunteers to write all of this stuff down? Amanda, you look like you want something to do." She gave me a dirty look, but she took my pad and pencil and at the top of a clean page she wrote, "Objective Statement." "Okay," she said to the group, "how do we want to word this?"

Mark said, "Just like Sheila put it a minute ago. We have this opportunity with the WindSailor, but we can't take advantage of it because..." Here he trailed off. "Why can't we take advantage of it?

It seems like we're going to. Isn't that what this whole project—"

Alice interrupted him. "Assignment."

"Yeah, assignment, is about?"

Sheila was way ahead of him. "We can't take advantage because we don't have the physical facilities, people, or systems to make the thing, and we don't have a marketing plan."

"Remember," I interjected, "the marketing plan isn't part of our assignment. That's Leslie's job."

"Hang on a minute," Amanda told us, "and let me get this down." We all waited as she scribbled furiously. When she was done, she read it back to us. "What is wrong with the existing situation? Hyler does not have the plant capacity, people, or systems to support its intention to take advantage of the opportunity created by the introduction of the WindSailor product."

We all thought for a minute. Then Mark said, "From our perspective, that's exactly what's wrong right now."

"Everyone okay with that?" I asked. They all nodded and I helped myself to a donut hole. "The next question is: How will things be better when we are done?"

"What's the point of this one?" Amanda asked. "The answer is just the opposite of the answer to the last one."

"I'm not sure," I said, "but let's stick with the questions. Our consultant had something in mind. Let's not break the pattern until we really understand it."

Everyone agreed, and Amanda wrote for a few moments before reading back to us: "How will things be better when we finish? The manufacturing capacity, along with the trained workers and administrative support systems, will be in place, and Hyler will be able to start producing the WindSailor, along with all of its other products."

When I heard this answer out loud, I started to have some ideas about why the question was there. But I decided to wait until we were finished the objective statement before saying anything.

Everyone agreed that Amanda's summary sounded pretty good, so I went on to the next question. "What are the performance criteria?" I looked up at the group. "The consultant said that the answer here should describe how the final product has to perform when the assignment is done."

We all looked at each other. I, for one, found this question tough because our product was somewhat intangible. I had another donut hole to hide my ignorance.

Alice said, "If our final product is to be an expanded manufacturing facility, a trained workforce, and all the systems to support it, the performance criterion is simple: the new facility, people, and systems must be capable of producing some number of WindSailors of appropriate quality."

Everyone nodded. "Will," Mark asked me, "How many of these things do they want us to make?"

I flipped through my notes. "Looks like 2,600 in the first year, and 6,000 per year after that."

Amanda wrote as I was reading the numbers out, and read back to us: "What are the performance criteria? Hyler must be capable of producing 2,600 WindSailors in the first year of production, and 6,000 in the second year."

Everybody else seemed to agree, except Luigi. "I think we need some performance criteria in there about the workers," he said.

"What did you have in mind?"

"Something about their ability to work with this manufacturing process. Don't forget, this is new to all of us. If it's coming from Germany, we can't afford to be flying technicians over here every time something breaks down."

We all looked at Amanda. "Summarize that in ten words or less," I told her. Her result was more than ten words, but we all liked it anyway. "The workers must be fully conversant with the manufacturing process for the WindSailor such that we do not require outside technical support after the WindSailor has gone into production."

Luigi was satisfied, and nobody had anything else to add to the performance criteria, so I went on to the next question: "What is the scope of the assignment?"

Leslie answered without hesitation. "Our scope is to make the WindSailor successful. That is what we are all here for."

Sheila did not agree. "That may be our hope, but really, our scope is all the work that gets the company ready to manufacture the WindSailors."

Luigi nodded. "There's a whole bunch of other work that goes into making this thing a success, like your marketing project." Here he looked over at me and said, "Sorry, your marketing assignment. Anyway, we don't want to lose focus on our work. Let's keep our scope to the work that needs to be done to get this thing ready for manufacturing."

Everyone except Leslie was happy with this. "I still don't think that's right, but it's your project. I'm just here as a liaison."

"How detailed should we get, Will?" Mark asked me. As if I knew. I answered anyway.

"Right now, we want to keep it to some broad statements about the work. We'll figure out the details later."

"For starters," Mark began, "there is hiring and training."

"Purchase of new equipment," added Luigi.

"Design and construction of new buildings," said Sheila.

"Upgrading old information systems, or designing new ones," said Amanda as she wrote down the points. We waited while Amanda finished writing. No one volunteered any more scope items.

I said, "I think that about covers it. Anything else will be too much detail."

"Let's just add one more statement, to kind of tie things up," Alice said. "Let's say something like: and all other activities related to preparing the WindSailor for hand over to production. That spells out even more clearly where the end of the assignment is, for us at least." Amanda dutifully wrote it down.

"What about marketing?" Sheila asked.

"Our group is taking care of all of that," Leslie told her.

"Marketing is separate, sure, it's just that I think we should mention that fact in our scope. Something to the effect that Marketing is NOT included."

"What's the point of that?" Mark asked. "If we try and list everything that isn't in this assignment, we'll be here for weeks!"

I agreed with Mark, but Sheila seemed to have a good handle on what we were doing so far, so I asked her to explain.

"In other projects I've worked on, there has often been a key activity or bit of information that had to come from outside our scope that we needed to continue with the project. If it was late, or the other people hadn't done their job right, it delayed our project. Then the sponsor wanted to know why we were behind. So if we let Stu know for certain what is not part of our assignment, he can make sure those things are ready for us."

There was only one problem that I could see. "Sheila, I don't see us having anything to do with Marketing. Other than getting the WindSailor ready for production in time."

"The look," Leslie said.

"Of course!" chimed in Luigi. "Good thing to think about now."

I felt left out. "Would someone please explain this to me?"

Luigi did the honors. "Part of what Leslie will be doing is coming up with a logo and colors and who knows what other artwork for the Hyler version of a WindSailor. All of that stuff is produced by Marketing."

"So?" I said.

"So, in case you forgot, part of that manufacturing process includes painting, decorating, and displaying the logo and product name prominently on each board. And before we can buy the paints, order the molds and templates, and train the painters, we need to know what this thing is going to be called, and what the graphic layout looks like."

Sheila said, "Thanks, Leslie. That's exactly what I meant, and it's all Marketing's responsibility. At some point, we're going to need that information, or else we won't be able to continue."

Amanda, who had been busy writing, waved her pad of paper and said, "How's this? The scope of this assignment specifically excludes all marketing related activities including the development of the product name and decoration."

I could tell that things were flowing smoothly because we were out of donut holes. Mark got up to get some more, and I read the next question. "What are the other constraints? These are things like time, cost, and quality. I'll start because Stu told me the total cost of the project will not exceed $1 million."

"Where did he get that number?" Sheila asked a little skeptically.

"Thin air probably. Or maybe it came out of Ralph's head." I was tempted to add it was the same thing.

"I really doubt they're making it up," Alice jumped in. "And I think it makes sense to put down what the constraints are. Then, when we have a better idea about how much this will all cost, we'll know where we started from."

This sounded like accounting reasoning to me, although I agreed for a different reason. "We're going to record all the constraints we know about. If the management group wants to impose constraints, so be it, but I don't intend to withhold any information to keep their egos intact. If their estimates are off the wall, I want them to know about it."

"We also know the schedule," said Luigi. "We have to be ready to produce these things by the middle of June." The way he said it hinted he didn't think we would be ready in time.

"I've got one that I bet no one has thought about," Amanda volunteered. "I'll bet that we have to maintain access to Hyler Lake during the whole assignment."

She was right. I certainly had not thought about that, and from the looks of the others, none of them had either. The Hyler plant is situated just outside of Enderby, next to a beautiful 130-acre freshwater lake. The town fathers had been farsighted back when Andrew Hyler wanted to build the original factory and agreed to let Hyler have the site, but they required him to build and maintain a public access to the lake. This proved to be a well-liked move (at least by the townspeople); Hyler Lake was a popular place for picnics, swimming, sailing, and fishing. Today, the lake is just as popular, and it fits our business. Because it is situated in a valley, the winds blow moderately and consistently all year round. We hold windsurfing races and sailboat regattas most weekends in the summer, and we use the lake as a testing ground for all our new products. The lake is the main reason we have a successful retail outlet at the plant site.

Having said all that, the lake is also a bit of an inconvenience. Our manufacturing facility is spread out among several buildings, and public access to the lake is right through the plant site. This means we have to maintain a security guard 24 hours a day, seven days a week, to make sure the public does not get too friendly with our stuff. And we have to put up with the "civilian" traffic around the factory.

The original plant was all in one building. At that time, Andrew Hyler thought it simpler to extend the road that went to the plant parking lot until it reached the edge of the lake. Hyler did not want to pay to put in a new access because this would have meant crossing a small creek and spending more money. That set-up worked until the plant started to expand, but since Hyler had agreed when he built the plant that it was his responsibility to provide a road, the town fathers were not about to let him back out of that promise. Out of stubbornness, or just plain cheapness, Hyler did not build a new road. He simply expanded the plant around the access road.

"Put it down," I told Amanda. "Although that gives us a whole new set of headaches."

"Cheer up," Mark told me. "Maybe this project will finally get the company to put in a separate public access." I could imagine a hundred other things that might get tacked onto this project.

Amanda read out, "Public access to Hyler Lake must be maintained during the assignment. How does that sound?"

"Are we done yet, Will?" Leslie asked me. "It's past 3:30, and I have some phone calls to make before the end of the day."

"Just three more questions," I told her. "The first is: Who is the sponsor?"

Sheila seemed to have a knack for all of this, because she asked, "How are you defining sponsor, exactly? That word gets as much abuse as the word project."

"The consultant said that the true sponsor is the person who is paying the bills, the person supplying the funding."

Mark said, "But that's not how it works at Hyler. Sponsors usually don't have any spending authority, but they deal with the person who does."

"You mean, that's how it doesn't work," Sheila retorted. "Whenever something comes up, we have to wait for the sponsor to ask the person who can actually decide. And then, since the real decision-makers haven't been close to the project, they usually decide the wrong thing. And guess what? It always turns out to be the project manager's fault when that bad decision screws up the schedule or the cost." She turned to me. "Let's put the responsibility where it belongs."

The only problem was, I had already been told who the sponsor was: Stu Barnes.

Amanda was quick to point this out. "Does Stu have spending authority on this assignment?"

"No. In fact, he specifically said that I would need Ralph's approval of all funding." I didn't like the way this was going.

Sheila did, though. "That's it, then. Ralph Borsellino is the sponsor."

I wasn't so sure. "Hold on a minute. What do the rest of you think?" I looked around the table.

"If we're going to use your consultant's framework, I think we have to follow his rules," Luigi said. "How else can we expect his ideas to work? I say Ralph's name should go on this thing."

"I agree," Mark said. "Ralph fits the definition."

"But, guys," I said, "do you have any idea of what it will be like having to deal with Ralph?"

Sheila was not sympathetic. "Ralph is the ultimate decisionmaker whether we call him the sponsor or not. If we're clear about his role up front, maybe we can avoid the difficulties we've all run into before when the real sponsor is removed from the assignment." I couldn't disagree with the logic, though I really would have preferred to have Stu deal with Ralph.

"Okay, Amanda," I gave in, "put it down." Then I said, "Last questions: Who is the project manager and what authority is being given?"

"That's an easy one," said Alice. "You are the project manager. And if Ralph is the sponsor, you won't have any authority." She smirked, but I knew she was only half-kidding.

Once again, Sheila jumped in. "Why not put down that the sponsor must approve the completion of each phase, and the plans for the next one? That way, we'll keep the sponsor up-to-date on exactly what's happening, and if he has a problem, he can let us know before the assignment progresses any further."

I started wondering whether I could get Sheila to take over as project manager. I didn't think it was likely, so I only said, "Okay, let's put something in about getting the sponsor's approval for expenditures over $50,000. Ralph will like that."

Amanda wrote and then read, "The sponsor of this assignment is Ralph Borsellino, president of Hyler Recreation Systems. The project manager is Will Campbell. He will report on the progress of the assignment in a bi-weekly meeting, and will get the sponsor's written approval to proceed at the completion of each phase. The project manager must also get approval for all expenditures over $50,000, and approval of on-going costs will be provided at the bi weekly progress meetings." She looked around at us. "I put in the part about the progress meetings on my own, but I think that would be a good idea." We all nodded in agreement.

Amanda ripped the top two pages off her pad and handed them to me. "There you go. Now what happens?"

"Now," I said, "I have to present this to the Hyler board of directors, and I have to get Ralph's signature at the bottom, giving the approval to proceed." Everyone looked at me sympathetically. Then they all got up to leave.

"Good luck!" said Luigi. "You're going to need it."

8

The Project Manager Faces the Board

I stayed behind and got myself another coffee and a chocolate chip cookie and thought about how different our objective statement was from the project goals we had developed that morning. Those goals had been vague and, as it turned out, not even all that accurate. Our assignment was not to make the WindSailor successful, it was just to build the facilities.

Something else I had learned: there was a big difference between the objective of the assignment (building the facilities), and the expected outcome or benefits (the success of the WindSailor). It appeared to be very important not to confuse one with the other, because you really only had control over achieving your objective. The expected benefit could only happen if the objective was achieved. Even then, your expectations might not be met if your objective was wrong in the first place. Fortunately, the WindSailor being a good idea was a strategic planning concern. I just had to get Hyler ready to make the thing.

On the whole, the objective statement approach had provided a concise definition of our assignment and a much better starting point. I was finally starting to feel comfortable with Martha's ideas.

The Board Has Questions

A little over 24 hours later, I was not feeling quite so comfortable. I was in the Ambassador Room at the Four Seasons Hotel in Portland, standing in front of the Hyler board of directors.

"And so you can see," I told them as I concluded my presentation, "the assignment has been clearly specified, the constraints noted, and the people playing the essential roles of project manager and sponsor identified. All we need now is approval from the sponsor to proceed ahead into the design." I stopped, looked around the room, and then sat down. Nobody said anything for a few minutes.

Finally Ralph spoke up. "I'm not sure I'm comfortable with that objective, Will. What about the WindSailor being a success?"

I was ready for that question, and I tried not too sound too confrontational. "The thing is, I don't think this assignment has the success of the WindSailor as its objective." That raised a few eyebrows around the table. "We're just preparing the facilities and the people to manufacture it, that's all."

"I find that a little hard to believe." This comment came from Leon Goldberg, a VP at Mantec. "Surely everyone involved with this project," I winced every time someone used that word—"has responsibility for the success of the WindSailor." A quick survey of faces indicated general agreement about this.

"Don't misunderstand me, Mr. Goldberg," I assured him. "I'm not saying that I don't have some responsibility for the success of the WindSailor. It's just that Hyler will have a better chance of achieving that objective if my project team identifies exactly what our piece of the puzzle is. Someone has already decided that the WindSailor has potential, and they have identified what needs to be done to exploit that potential. My assignment is only one piece of all that. The product needs to be marketed, contracts need to be negotiated, all kinds of things need to be done in addition to upgrading our facilities. Our piece alone is not enough to achieve the overall objective. Consequently, we don't want to assume responsibility for the WindSailor's success because we can't achieve it by ourselves. It makes more sense for us to focus on our piece."

I could tell Ralph was not happy with this response, but the other board members, and especially Henry Stanton, the president of Mantec, were nodding. Mentally I scored one for the good guys.

Ralph wasn't ready to quit yet. "You identified me as the sponsor of this project, but I specifically named Stu Barnes." He gestured at Stu who was sitting beside him. "I did that because I won't have enough time to devote to this project. Why did you change that?"

Ralph was out to embarrass himself. I had no intention of doing the same on my behalf. "Ralph, you also specified that all spending decisions would have to be approved by you."

Ralph interrupted. "That's exactly right." He looked around the table at the other board members. "I'm responsible for this division, so I approve whatever gets spent." He seemed to be assuring everyone that he was in control.

I didn't get a chance to continue because Carrie Starblanket spoke up. She was the vice-president of marketing at Hyler. She had an unusual last name because her father was Navaho. "Ralph, if you want to have approval over all the money decisions on this project, what do you want Stuart to do?"

Good question! Ralph hesitated a bit before answering. "He will help the project manager get necessary resources." He paused. "And act as my liaison with the project team."

James Graubard, president of a local public relations firm, and the only board member from outside Mantec asked another question. "Having Stuart around seems like an unnecessary layer."

Ralph looked peeved. "I told you, I don't have time to sponsor this project. Besides, Stu is much more familiar with the whole thing that I am."

Graubard said, "But it seems to me that before you can approve any spending, you will need a detailed understanding of what you're deciding on, won't you?"

"Not really," Ralph answered. "I run a pretty self-empowered management team. I trust Stu, and I would normally go with what Stu recommends." As soon as he said it, he realized his mistake.

Graubard asked him anyway. "So why don't you just remove that extra step and give Stuart spending authority?"

Ralph squirmed a bit in his chair. "This is an important project. I need to keep my finger on it."

Lou Teves, another VP at Mantec chimed in, "But you just told us that you will probably take Stuart's recommendations about spending decisions."

Henry Stanton finally spoke up. "Ralph, you appear to have two choices: delegate spending authority to Stu and make him a true sponsor, or make the time to be a proper sponsor yourself."

Beautiful! I couldn't believe it had worked out so well. Best of all, I hadn't had to say anything to get them all to the conclusion I wanted, so Ralph couldn't blame me for what happened. Or so I thought.

Ralph was flipping madly through his diary, checking, I assumed, to see if he had time to be part of this assignment. Finally, he said, "I guess I'll make time to sponsor it." He didn't look too happy.

The Project Has a Sponsor

Henry Stanton looked pleased. "I think that is the right choice, Ralph. This is the most important new product that Hyler has taken on in some time. I think it requires your involvement." Ralph looked somewhat mollified. "But that leaves a question," Stanton continued. "Where does Stuart fit into this assignment? It was his idea to take on this product." Everyone looked around the table at each other until all their eyes ended up on me.

An important lesson I have learned in life is that if you are asked a question in a roomful of people and you don't know the answer, never confess ignorance. Instead, look thoughtful and stall, because someone else will almost always volunteer something you can use. I followed my own advice and I was not disappointed.

"I'll act as a business analyst," Stu volunteered. "I did the original feasibility analysis and laid out the general parameters of both this project and the marketing one. I can advise Ralph about the effect of his decisions on the success of the product."

Everyone seemed to think that this was a good idea, including me. I wanted Stu to be involved.

Ralph had one more question for me. "Have you got a schedule of the work yet? Or a work breakdown structure to show us?"

Honesty seemed to be working well for me, so I told him, "Actually, I don't have those yet."

This was not strictly true. At 9:00 a.m. Al Burton had presented me with a list of his tasks, a work breakdown structure chart, and a schedule for his work. After looking it over, I asked him why he was planning an entirely new building south of our existing plant. I had thought that expanding our current facilities would be cheaper.

"It's what Ralph wants," Al told me, a little peevishly. "He doesn't want to add on to this dilapidated factory. He wants a whole new facility for the WindSailor."

I was instantly full of questions. "Can we afford a new building? And have you consulted with Luigi in Production? What about the inventory people?" Al must have thought I was not confident in his work.

"We'll go over all of that stuff later," he told me. "If people want to change it, we'll change it. Meanwhile, you'll need this schedule for you presentation."

I had a problem with Al's logic. "I don't feel comfortable committing to a schedule when we haven't decided what we are going to build."

This flustered Al. "It has to be done by June next year, right?"

"That's the deadline we've been given," I confirmed.

"Well, this schedule fits in that time frame, and that's all that matters!"

As Al got more upset, so did I. "Wouldn't it make just a bit more sense to figure out how long it will actually take, and then look at our time constraints? Look what happened in Europe! They missed their window by months!"

Al leaned over my desk. "You just don't know much about projects do you?" He didn't wait for an answer, just turned and left my office.

Setting the Schedule

I nudged myself out of my reverie about Al, and concentrated on Ralph's question. "Ralph, we don't have a schedule yet because we don't know exactly what we are doing yet."

It was perhaps not the best choice of words. "You see, we have to be able to produce WindSailors, but we still need to determine the best way to do that. For example, do we expand our current plant facilities, or build an entirely new, separate building?"

Jeannie Granato sounded incredulous. "You have to go to production by June and you don't know how you are going to do it yet?" I wasn't sure just what Jeannie did at Mantec, but it sounded like it was probably annoying.

As calmly as I could, I said, "The time constraints will certainly influence how we decide to expand. Once I get approval to proceed, that will be my next step." I hoped that I was understanding what Martha meant by the design phase. "To get the best final product, we need to take the assignment one step at a time, starting with the objective statement. Once we have that, we can figure out the best way to do it."

Ms. Granato did not look convinced. Ralph didn't help things when he said, "Can you give us an estimate on how long the design will take?"

I honestly did not know, so I told them. "I spoke with one of the designers this morning, and he told me that it will depend which option we go with. It might take three weeks or it might take two months."

Almost everyone was looking uncomfortable. Fortunately, one of the board members came to my rescue.

"Mr. Campbell is perfectly correct in not giving you a firm date for completing the design." My savior was Graubard. "I've worked in public relations and advertising for 30 years now, and that business is almost all design. Anytime someone puts a firm time frame on how long it will take, I get worried. Design is a creative process. I've never been very successful in keeping it to a firm schedule. How long does it take to come up with a good idea?"

This did not satisfy Granato. "But this whole project has to be completed by June! How can we be sure it's going to get done?"

"How long will the actual construction, and hiring and training of personnel take?" Ralph asked me. I couldn't believe it! He was missing the whole point.

"I can't tell you that until we know what we're building Ralph," I said. "A new building will take longer than just expanding. When we've finished the design, we'll have a better idea." After I said it, I realized that I had often told people how long something would take before I knew exactly what it was. For some reason, I was hardly ever right.

Graubard backed me up again. "Our marketing experts have given us their best guess about when this product has to be ready, but just because we want that to happen doesn't mean that it will." He turned to me and said, "I'm glad you're not giving us a firm deadline."

Henry Stanton stepped in to close down the discussion on this point. "Will, keep your sponsor informed, and as soon as you can estimate a completion date, get the sponsor's approval."

Ms. Granato asked, "What if his estimate is later than our June deadline?"

Stanton responded, "There is always a trade off between time and money, Jeanie. I'm sure that our project manager and sponsor will figure out a way. They may have to spend more money." Later, I was very glad about that comment, and the fact that Mantec's president had made it.

After that, I had to tell the board about why we would have to maintain public access to Lake Hyler. Then Ralph signed the objective statement, right there in front of everyone. He also made me sign it, but that didn't make me uncomfortable at all.

The board was then ready for the next item: a presentation by Leslie Frame and Carrie Starblanket on marketing the WindSailor. I wished Leslie luck as I passed her on the way out.

Part Two

The
Project
Team

9

The Team's Roles

"I thought you said design was the next step."

It was the evening after the board meeting, and I was back in what was quickly becoming my accustomed spot on the front porch of my in-laws' house.

"How do you expect to play a round of golf if you don't know what clubs you've got?" Martha snapped. She was in a bad mood today. "You can't go on to the next step until you know who is supposed to do what on your project team!"

"Wait a minute, Martha," I said. "I thought you told me that the golf clubs were like the planning tools that I was going to use."

"I also told you I don't like analogies. Forget about the golf clubs. But you can't go on to the next step until you know who does what!" She passed me the notepad on which she had written:

SPONSOR
FEASIBILITY ANALYST
PROJECT MANAGER ⎫
DESIGNER ⎪
IMPLEMENTOR ⎬ THE TEAM
USERS' REPRESENTATIVE ⎪
ADMINISTRATOR ⎭
REVIEWERS

"That doesn't look like a lot of people, Martha," I said. "I think there will be a lot more than that on my pro—, I mean, assignment."

"If you would just let me explain, Willie! There are certain responsibilities that need to be fulfilled during every assignment, big or small. These responsibilities are easier to think about when we group similar ones together, and give each group a name. On a small assignment, the same person might play more than one role. And on a big assignment—"

"You might have many people filling one particular area of responsibility," I finished for her. "That makes more sense."

Martha continued as if I hadn't interrupted. "On a bigger assignment, with many people in a single role, it is important to have one person in charge of each role." That sounded logical. Just like you only want one project manager, you would probably want one person in charge of the design process, even if a lot of people were working on it. And the whole thing would be much easier to coordinate that way. Martha stared at me over the top of her glasses. "Please note, Will, this is *not* a committee!"

I decided not to question that remark and said, "So I guess we need to define these roles with detailed job descriptions," I trailed off as Martha sneered at me.

"That is exactly what we don't want to do," she told me. "Think about the roles in terms of what they must contribute to the assignment. That way, you don't restrict what they do." I wasn't sure I understood that, but Martha looked too cranky for me to ask for an explanation.

The Sponsor

She pointed to the sponsor first. "We already talked about this one. What does he or she contribute?"

How I could I forget? "In my case it's a he, and he is supposed to contribute the money."

"And all the responsibility that goes with it," Martha finished for me. "Since he is paying, the sponsor can decide everything. Of course, a good sponsor doesn't want to do that, which is why he hires a project manager. However, the basic framework of an assignment provides the sponsor with neat, controlled opportunities to provide his approval. At the very minimum, you should get the sponsor's signed approval of the just-completed phase, and the agreement to continue on."

I was thinking of Ralph and I wasn't so sure. If Ralph had to sign-off on each phase, he would be very aware of what had happened so far, and how this would affect the future of the assignment. It was obvious: if he understood the current state of the assignment, the sponsor would be in a much better position to make decisions about the future of the assignment. I told Martha this. "Correct," she said. "You learn more and more about how your assignment will turn out as you get further and further along. By the end, you know everything there is to know, except it's a little too late to help you. So as you go, you want the sponsor to be continually aware of what the situation is. The end of each phase happens to provide an ideal point for review. For example, what will you have a better idea about once you finish all the design work for your assignment?"

"How much it will cost and how long it will take."

Martha wasn't quite satisfied with that. "You'll have a better idea about those things, Willie," she said. "You won't know them in detail until after the execution planning phase. Now what would your sponsor do if instead of $1 million, you estimated your assignment would cost $5 million to complete?"

I didn't have to think about that one for very long. "He'd probably stop the project."

"He might," Martha allowed. "What he should do is ask his feasibility analyst to see if the assignment is still justified at that cost. If it isn't, he should stop the project." She took a pull on her pipe and blew a smoke ring out over the porch railing. It was a still evening so the ring hung together for a long time as it floated out over the lawn.

"The point is, when you finish a phase of the assignment, you have more information. The sponsor needs to be aware of the information because he needs to decide how to proceed with the assignment. Far too many assignments build up their own momentum, and continue long after they no longer make sense."

The Feasibility Analyst

"What about the feasibility analyst?" I asked Martha. "My boss, the person who started this whole WindSailor thing, volunteered to play that role. Although he used a slightly different name, I'm sure it's the same thing."

"What do you think your boss will be doing on this assignment?" Martha asked.

I thought back to what Stu told the board yesterday. "He'll be advising the sponsor on the viability of the assignment as we go along."

"That is exactly what a feasibility analyst does. He provides the sponsor with an objective assessment, usually from a financial perspective."

"Why not have the project manager do this?" I asked. "He's right in on the action."

"How objective do you think the project manager is likely to be after the assignment begins?" Martha asked.

Good point, I thought. I'd probably stop wondering whether the assignment was a good idea and narrow my focus to thinking a lot more about how to accomplish it.

Martha didn't wait for me to answer. "As I said before, on a smaller assignment, this might not be a separate person. But on something the size of your assignment, an objective feasibility analyst is an asset."

The Project Manager

Martha picked up her pencil and tapped the next name on the list. "What about the project manager? What are you supposed to contribute?"

That was easy. "The finished product, as it was spelled out in the objective statement. I get to do all of the actual work."

Martha nodded. "That's essentially it. Of course, good communication with your sponsor and good planning techniques, as well as lots of performance management tricks, will help you to deliver the product, but you'll find out more about those later." It sounded like a lot of work to me.

The Designer, Implementer, User's Representative, and Project Administrator

We continued on, one by one. The designer was to coordinate the production of the design. The implementer was the person "on the ground" who built the product. The user's representative was supposed to canvass the people who had to live with the finished product and convey their interests to the project team, and especially to the designer.

"A very misunderstood role," Martha told me about the user's representative. "It requires a lot of work, because there are often many users, with a wide variety of requirements, for every assignment. Frequently this is ignored, and no one is happy with the final product. No matter how good your idea is, if you don't accommodate the users, it can be unworkable in reality."

The project administrator, according to Martha, was also an unsung hero of the project team. "It takes a special kind of concentration to keep schedules up to date, keep everyone informed of progress, produce reports, keep track of costs, and do all those important things that so often get neglected. No wonder so many projects go over budget and take too long. Everyone is too busy doing other things to keep track of where they are!"

Martha suggested we leave the reviewer's role to discuss later, and then she started coughing. Martha gets these funny spells where she coughs and coughs, to the point where you think one of her lungs is about to come up and land on the floor in front of you. Her doctor says it's because of her pipe smoking, but Martha has no intention of giving that up.

I called Natalie and we carried Martha inside and to her bedroom. Fortunately, her room is on the ground floor, because Martha is not the lightest person I have ever tried to carry off to bed. After that, I just felt I was getting underfoot, so I said my goodnights. Even from the driveway I could hear her, still hacking away.

As I started my car, I had a very selfish thought: I hoped she wouldn't die before she finished telling me about projects.

A Contest of Convictions

"Why don't you get the first round, Will? You can just bill it to the project." Al gave me a weak smile to go with his weak joke. I got up and pushed my way through the crowd to buy the drinks. It serves me right for being so keen, I thought.

As soon as I had arrived home from visiting Martha I called my project team to set up an early meeting the next day. I wanted to waste no time in identifying who would be who on the project. Instead of simply agreeing to be there, Al had insisted that the two of us get together, now, that same night. There were important issues, he said. It had been a very long day and here I was standing at the bar of an English style pub called the Gasping Goose or the Twisted Chicken, ordering a couple of mugs of some strange English-style brew. As I returned to the table, I spilled beer on three different people. Nobody seemed to mind.

"Here you go Al," I said, sliding him a mug of something called Ruddles Bitter. We sat silently regarding our beer for a few minutes until I could stand it no longer. "So what was it you wanted to talk about?"

"My first job out of college was assistant supervisor of a drilling crew on an oil rig. Al took a sip of his beer. "Armadillo Oil was the company. Down in Texas. I was fresh out of college with my shiny new engineering degree and they put me in charge of a bunch of roughnecks. Know what happened?"

I tried my beer. It had a thick, bitter taste and it didn't seem to be carbonated. It was also warm. "No," I told him.

Al laughed. "They just about tore me apart. Literally. Ever work around an oil rig, Will? No? Well let me tell you, a rig is a very dangerous place to be, especially if you're an uppity young college graduate who is supposed to be the boss. There's a hundred ways to lose a hand, an arm, or your life. Those guys pulled every trick in the book on me. It took a while for me to figure out that they knew what they were doing and that I should learn from them, not tell them how to do it. Things went much better after I got that through my head. I spent ten years working in the oil industry, places all over the world. Spent some time up in the North Sea, which is where I got to know this beer. But I never forgot the lesson I learned back in Texas."

I took another sip of the beer and began wondering if those Texan roughnecks had removed Al's taste buds. "What exactly was it that you learned in Texas?"

Al looked up at me for the first time since I brought the beer over. "The same lesson you need to learn right now Will: that you don't know it all; that others have gone before you and picked up a trick or two; that if you try and figure everything out for yourself you'll end up looking silly in the best case, and in a downright bad situation in the worst case!"

We had obviously moved a long way from armadillos and cute pranks involving hand loss. "I'm not sure I understand what you mean."

He gave me an exasperated look. When he spoke his voice was high and tense. "Do you know how long I've been managing projects? Over twenty years! Don't you think that just maybe, between me and all of my colleagues, we might have some good ideas about how to make a project run smoothly?"

"Of course Al," I said, hoping to placate him somewhat.

"It's bad enough having Stuart Barnes insist that someone as inexperienced as you take on the WindSailor, but you continually question everything I tell you. Why is it so hard for you to accept that I might be right?"

I tried to sound non-threatening. "It's not that I don't trust you, it's just that I want to try and find an even better way of doing things. And besides," I added, perhaps foolishly, "I don't think that your ideas work in every situation."

"You don't think that work breakdown structures are useful? You don't think that earned value costing, which is endorsed by the United States Government, is useful?"

I tried a different tack. "That's not what I'm saying at all, Al. I just want to work out each move logically before we do anything."

"You haven't got any experience."

I tried to be conciliatory. "Don't forget, I'm also relying on my consultant's experience."

"That's the thing that bugs me the most, Will! There isn't any consultant. I checked with Ralph, and he hasn't authorized any money for any consultant. So that's how I know you're doing it all yourself. You just think your ideas will have more impact with the project team if you tell them a consultant came up with them."

I tried to change the subject. "I think parts of your approach work, Al, but I need to think out my approach to projects from the basics."

Al leaned back in his chair. "Look Will, the WindSailor is a big deal for Hyler. We can't afford to have you trying out your pet theories about project management on something so vital. Go with the conventional wisdom on this one."

I tried to keep my tone as calm and reasonable as Al's. "Let's suppose you have an important job. Let's also suppose that a standard method for doing the job exists, but that method was not a very good one. It wasn't completely wrong, but it wasn't a good way of doing the job, even though many people and many books supported that method. Now pretend you've worked out a new way of doing the job. You figure this new method will produce much better results. You've never tried the new way, but you've thought about it very carefully, and you're as certain as you can be that it will work better than the old way. Which way would you do the job?"

"As a responsible manager, I would have to do it the accepted way."

"But Al," I exploded. "The old way isn't any good!"

Al took another sip of his beer. "You missed the whole point of the oil rig story didn't you, Will? I told you, other people have been there before you. They've probably already tried all of your hare-brained ideas, but they're not using them, because they don't work."

Biting back a nasty reply I said, "If we can't use logic to come to agreement on things, how are we going to get along?"

"Will, experience is the best teacher." He drank the last of his beer. "It's getting late. Are you going to stick to accepted project management principles on this?"

I shook my head. "Al, I have to keep questioning things I don't agree with. Think of it this way: if the things I question actually do make sense, you'll have no trouble explaining them to me."

Al gave me a cold look. "I don't have anymore time for this." He grabbed his coat and stalked off toward the door.

"See you in the morning?" I called after his departing back.

Assigning the Roles

Sleepy eyes greeted me at the donut shop at 7:00 a.m. the next morning.

"Couldn't this have waited for a more reasonable hour?" moaned Mark. He was the kind of guy who had a hard time being at his desk before 9 a.m., but everybody else agreed. Except for Al who hadn't shown up yet.

"Afraid not folks," I told them. "But look at the bounty nature provides when you rise early!" I pointed to the tray of danishes in the center of the table, and the large pot of coffee. "Eat, drink, and think along with me now, as we try and figure out the next move." I began by telling the group about the presentation to the Hyler board of directors, and how our objective statement had been signed off by Ralph. Everyone was pleased about that, so I went on to talk about roles and responsibilities on the project team.

I had arrived even earlier in the day and written on a sheet of paper all the roles Martha and I had discussed. I put that out on the table in front of everyone and gave them a brief synopsis of what my "consultant" had been telling me.

"How can you have just one user's rep?" Alice asked. "There are a lot of people, especially on this project, that need to be involved. Maybe we should have a committee of users."

The word committee always makes me nervous. I was not alone. "Have you ever tried to work with a committee?" Sheila asked her.

"I realize that," said Alice, "but how else are you going to hear all of the users' concerns?"

I stepped in. "My consultant said that we need to have one person on the project team who is in charge of each role, but the user's rep, for example, might organize a committee of users. However, it's the user's rep, not the committee, who works with the project team." We deal only with the team member, not the 150 people they talk to in order to get their information."

"That setup works well," Leslie told us. "When we contract for assistance in advertising campaigns, we only deal with one key contact. In fact, the contractors insist on it. They find it's the only way they can stay clear on exactly what we want."

Luigi said, "I'm not really clear on this implementer person. Aren't we going to be doing most of the actual work?"

"If we are, then I guess we'll be playing the role of implementer," I said. "But there may be others from outside the project team who do the actual work. We're going to have to hire a bunch of people to build the WindSailor. We might use a headhunter or employment agency to do that."

"I've got a better example," Sheila said. "When we do the construction work to expand the plant, we'll hire a construction contractor, and the contractor will supply a person who will look at our design and then direct the people and equipment to construct the plant to our design. That person would be an implementer."

I said, "So, now all we have to do is decide who gets to play which role."

It took us 30 minutes to finally divvy up the roles. In the end, the team looked like this:

Sponsor	Ralph Borsellino
Feasibility Analyst	Stu Barnes
Project Manager	Will Campbell
Designer	Al Burton
Implementer	Unsure, everyone?
Project Administrator	Sheila Chan
User's Rep	Amanda Payton

"You have to recognize that some of us will be involved in other areas," Sheila said. "I will be doing a lot of work with Al on design, and several of us will have to work on the implementation."

"And what about me and Leslie and Mark?" Luigi asked. "What are we supposed to be doing?"

"First of all, I don't think helping out with someone else's responsibility is a problem, so long as you remember what your primary role is. Secondly," I turned to Luigi, "I expect that you will be one of the implementers. You are one of the users, and you will be helping out on the design. Don't worry, there will be plenty for you to do. Same with you Leslie." I thought for a moment. "And besides, you two won't have to come to every one of these meetings." They were happy about that, and I decided to wrap things up.

"Okay, everyone, the next phase is design. My consultant is out of town for a few days, so we're going to tackle this one on our own. Amanda, you get together a list of the users so we know who we need to run the design by."

"What about our list of tasks and work breakdown structures?" Sheila asked. "The things we decided to do after the very first meeting."

"Let's forget about those for now," I told her. "I want to stick with the consultant's process."

"Look at that, people," I said, pointing at the clock over the donut counter. "Only 8:00 a.m. You've still got the whole day ahead of you! We'll have to do this more often."

Everyone rolled their eyes.

10

Company Politics

My feeling that things were finally under control should have been a signal that something bad was about to happen.

"Good morning, Mr. Early Bird." Stu was sitting at my desk, feet up. "And how is my project manager this morning?" I could tell by the way he said it that he was not in a good mood. " When you check your voice-mail, you'll find a personal request from Ralph himself to be in his office as soon as you get in. I recommend that you pay attention to it, because the Great One has requested my presence as well." He took his feet off the desk, stood up, and walked around it, planting himself right in front of me. Stu is about six inches taller than I am, and just then, it seemed like a big six inches. In his best drill-sergeant tone he said: "What the *hell* are you doing with this project, Will?"

It didn't seem like he wanted an answer, and he started to walk around behind me like he was talking to a marine recruit who was about to get an extra 200 pushups. "Remember Al?"

"Yes." I stifled the urge to add "sir." "You're the one who put him on my project team." That was not what Stu wanted to hear, because, still sounding like a movie drill sergeant, he said, "And you managed to get him *off* your project team!"

I listened as Stu gave me the facts in his rapid-fire manner. Apparently Al had complained to Ralph about how I was handling the WindSailor project. Last night, after our meeting at the Throttled Duck, he had called Ralph at home and demanded to see him face to face, and it couldn't wait until morning. Ralph was not all that happy about being disturbed at that hour, and he was even less happy when he heard what Al had to tell him.

California Water Sports Inc., a San Francisco competitor, had been talking to Al for some time about having him come to work for them. Al had repeatedly declined, he told Ralph, for a number of reasons including, he claimed, his loyalty to Hyler. Lately, though, Al hadn't been feeling appreciated, and not being made project manager for the WindSailor was the last straw. That an incompetent like me was put in charge indicated to Al that there was no longer any place for him at Hyler. He had accepted a job with the San Francisco company.

To be honest, I saw this news as cause for celebration. In fact, I figured I should be rewarded. I had managed to make Al leave of his own free will. This would help not only the WindSailor project, but all future work at Hyler. Maybe this project management stuff wasn't so bad after all!

Stu said, "Get that smart-ass grin off your face! You know damn well that if Al had been under my authority, I would have fired him long ago! But he wasn't. The point is, Ralph specifically chose him to be part of this project. It was one of the conditions I had to accept in order to get Ralph to go along with the WindSailor. And now you go and make him quit!"

I had to defend myself. "I was busting my butt to work with him, and he was doing nothing but trying to bring the whole WindSailor project down. He was the one trying to make me quit. He even told me so!"

"You just don't understand the politics. Al was Ralph's representative on the project team. When Al quits and says it's because you are cutting him out of the project, who do you think Ralph will believe?"

Stu motioned for me to sit, and he started to talk in a much calmer voice. "Look, Will, I know you didn't try to make this happen. It's just that I get a little frustrated sometimes because you like to ignore some realities." Personally, I thought the reality was that we were all better off without Al. Stu continued, "I think the WindSailor will be good for Hyler, so I'll do whatever it takes to make it happen. That means keeping Ralph happy while still getting the job done. Your part in this little drama was supposed to have been to keep Al happy. Or at least to keep him from quitting, and claiming you're incompetent. Can you see how a little thing like that might have an impact on Ralph and his opinion?"

When he put it that way, I allowed as how I might be able to understand it.

Stu sighed. "Well, now I want to tell you what will probably happen next. With Al gone, our illustrious president is going to be very concerned about his ability to keep his paws on this project. Negotiations with the WaterTrend people in Germany are at the point where we can't really back out of the deal, and luckily Ralph signed that objective form thing of yours in front of all the board members. This means that as much as he may not like to, Ralph will have to go ahead with the WindSailor. However, he will threaten to cancel the project and fire both of us before he lets us know that it will continue. Your job in this meeting will be to act humble, wrong, and very willing to do better in the future. I really don't care who's right. I want this project to go ahead." His face took on that army look again. "Do you understand?"

This time I couldn't resist. "Yes, sir," I told him.

Keeping the Sponsor Happy

"I should fire you on the spot! Al was here for five years before you showed up and after only two days in charge of this project, you manage to get him to quit!"

I was amazed. The scene was playing out exactly as Stu predicted. I tried to look humble and said, "I'm sorry it happened, Ralph." And then, because I really wasn't all that humble, I told him, "I was just trying to get the project done."

Ralph was not impressed. "Well you're going to have to try harder to get along with people!" Yeah, I thought, that was one of Al's strong suits. Ralph walked over to his office window overlooking the plant site. "Losing Al is a great detriment to our ability to complete this project and I have thought seriously about canceling the whole thing." I glanced at Stu with admiration. The man was a genius. He could read company politics like a road map.

Ralph sighed and put on an expression that truly made him look like a man of wisdom. "In the end, I concluded that this project is too important to the company." He turned back to both of us. "I want to continue on with it. But you," —here he looked at me— "are going to have to work on your people skills."

"By the way," he continued, "I like some things that you're doing, Will, but don't forget, you're supposed to meet with me regularly to bring me up-to-date." He went to his desk and flipped open his calendar. "Let's set a date right now. How's Tuesday?"

It was Thursday, the last day in August, and I wasn't sure I would have all that much to report by Tuesday, but I told him okay. It seemed the wisest move.

On that note, we were dismissed. As we walked down the hallway towards Stu's office, I had to express my reverence. "You called it exactly!" I slapped him on the back. "Man, am I impressed!"

Stu was not in the mood to celebrate. "You just don't understand, Will. You think that we're the good guys, and that Ralph is out to get us. That's just not true. Ralph is not such a bad guy. He really does want to do what's best for the company. It's just that he has to play the game like the rest of us." He stopped and turned to face me. "If you try to understand Ralph a little better, and then give him what he needs, he won't cause much trouble. If you expect him to simply know the right thing to do, you'll be allowing him to fail. This is not about being right or wrong or scoring points, Will. This is about making the WindSailor work. I want you to think about that."

Part Three

The Design Phase

11

What is Design, and How Long Does it Take?

"Quit?" Jenny asked me. "Just because of you?" Sometimes my wife has a way of making me feel inconsequential.

"Well, at least partly because of me," I told her, trying to preserve my place among the causes of Al Burton's resignation.

"Is anybody worried that he might help your competitor scoop you on the WindSailor?" My wife, always the cheerful one.

"No one seems too concerned," I told her. "My biggest concern is Martha's health." Her coughing fit of yesterday had led to a visit to the hospital today. The doctors said she just needed to rest, and to quit smoking her pipe. According to Natalie, this diagnosis had confirmed Martha's low opinion of the medical establishment.

"I've always told you that you'd get to like Martha if you just gave her a chance," Jenny said. I didn't bother to correct her about my true motive. "Mom told me to say that Martha would like to see you tomorrow if you're not too busy. She seems to be getting fond of you, too!" All this fondness was making Jenny very happy.

Just then my daughter came downstairs. "Daddy, Daddy, look at my ribbon. I won the chess tournament. I beat all of the older kids!" This was definitely good news and I picked her up and gave her a big hug.

Normal in every other way, Sarah became fascinated with chess when she was four. At first, I thought she just wanted to put the pieces in her mouth, but right from the beginning, she wanted to learn how to play, just like a grown-up. After two years, she didn't play it just like a grown-up, she played it better than most. Her skill level had reached the point where I would soon have to stop playing her or face defeat at the hands of a six year old.

"Everyone thought Alistair was going to win 'cause he's in grade six," she told me. "But I just concentrated like you told me and I beat him easy!"

"Easily, honey," my wife corrected. Jenny is determined that our kids will learn to speak correctly, chess geniuses or not. "Why don't you go wash up for dinner?"

"Daddy, will you play me after dinner?" Sarah asked. I told her I would play a game with her as soon as we cleaned up the dinner dishes.

As I helped Jenny set the table, I was deep in thought about the design process. I was comfortable with the idea that we couldn't do an execution plan and schedule until after we knew exactly what we were going to build. That now seemed obvious. My question was one I thought Martha would ask me: What is the result of the design phase? What do you have when you are completely finished? Ideas popped into my head: blue prints, drawings, diagrams, pictures, things you might have after you do a design. For the WindSailor assignment, we would need both new organization charts and blue prints. We would also need flow charts and other plans for the new software, and written specifications for any new hardware, not to mention a scheduling system, a manning document, standard method instructions, and many other items. There would be lots of ways to communicate the design on this assignment.

If the design phase produces plans or drawings or flow charts, what is it that they do? They are, after all, only ways of conveying what the design is. If I could answer this question, I would have the result of the design phase. The one thing they all had in common was that they were describing something: the final product. Each one of those tools was giving its own picture of exactly what the final product would look like, whether that product was a building, a department, or a software program.

Aha! I thought as I put the water glasses at each place setting, the process of design has to do with describing the product in detail. Therefore, the result of the design is a description of the product, detailed enough so you could build the thing, whatever it was.

Martha would have been proud of me. It was so obvious now, but I still felt like patting myself on the back.

> The design process describes the final product in enough detail so that you could produce it.

This led me to my next question. Graubard had said at the board meeting that design was hard to schedule. He said something about the process being creative and difficult to predict. But surely a good architect can tell you how long it takes to design a building. Why would it be uncertain?

"—the left side," my wife interrupted my thoughts.

"Sorry, hon, what was that?"

"I said, the forks go on the left side, not the right." She gave me a look of mock horror and helped me switch them back.

Dinner time conversation was taken up by talk of chess tournaments, and by Jake spilling his carrots all over the floor. Fortunately Max, our dog, has learned to lie underneath Jake's chair. He ate most of them before he realized that dogs aren't supposed to like vegetables.

When the dishes were cleared up and everything was back to its pre-supper state of disorder, Sarah reminded me of my promise.

"Time to play, Daddy," she told me.

"Don't worry, honey, I'll play. But I can't play for very long. I have some work to do tonight."

"Okay," she said excitedly. "Just until it's my bedtime." That was two hours from now.

"Forty-five minutes," I told her firmly, thinking that at about 20 minutes each, this would allow time for two games. With a little luck I could then get back to thinking about design, my ego still intact, at least until our next match.

Sarah held out her two fists. I tapped the right one, and she opened her hand. It contained a black pawn. "I get to play white." Sarah considered this to be a significant advantage. The chessboard was set up on the coffee table. I sat down on the couch and she sat cross legged on the floor opposite me. Suddenly my rambunctious little girl was gone, and in her place sat a serious-looking chess master. She picked up the pawn in front of her king and moved it two spaces ahead. I did the same with my king's pawn.

I should have been concentrating on the game in front of me. Instead, my mind started to wander back to design. Sarah moved her king's bishop diagonally across the black squares until it sat three spaces in front her other bishop.

Why should scheduling design be so tough? I asked myself. I thought back to my own experience with software design. I had often run into trouble, usually because the users kept changing their requirements. Every time we would complete something, they would add a requirement, and this caused endless delays. I moved my queen's knight to bishop three.

I would make sure we had the requirements clearly stated before we did any design work. That way we wouldn't have to put up with ongoing additions, and we could stick to our schedule. And I would make sure Ralph signed off on the design when it was complete, to try and minimize changes to the design during execution. Of course, that was built into Martha's process. Sarah moved her queen to bishop three.

If I could get a clear set of requirements for the design, which I had already started to do with the objective statement, and Ralph signed off the completed design, where was the problem? Why was scheduling design work so difficult? I moved my pawn to queen four and looked at my watch. Only three minutes gone. Sarah and I almost always took 20 minutes to play a game.

"Checkmate, Daddy!" Sarah said delightedly as she moved her queen to take the pawn in front of my king's bishop. "I won! I won! I beat Daddy!" She went streaking into the other room to tell her mother. It appeared some lessons in good sportsmanship were in order.

I must have been half asleep to let it happen, but she was my daughter, and I felt pretty proud of her. I could hear her giving her mother a play by play account of her victory. She told her mother she had used a variation on the Lopez opening, whatever that was.

Boy, I thought to myself, if I can't even predict how long a chess game with my daughter is going to take, no wonder people are thinking that I'll have trouble with design. I stared at the board and thought about it in a slightly different way.

"Sarah," I called to the next room, "C'mere, honey. I need to ask you a question."

Sarah came bouncing back into the room. "You're not mad, are you, Daddy? I mean, 'cause I beat you?" I tried not to smile too much. "Of course not, honey. I'm very proud of you." And I'll pay more attention next time, I thought to myself. "But I need your help." Sarah became serious again when I said this, concentrating like a chess master. "Sarah, how long does it take to play a game of chess?"

She looked puzzled. "It's different every time, Daddy," she told me. "Sometimes it takes a long time if I'm playing someone good, and sometimes it only takes a little while." I ignored the back-handed insult. "So why can't you tell how long a game will take?"

She thought about it for a minute. "Every game is different, Daddy."

"Do you have a plan in your head when you start a game?" I asked her.

"Yes, I do," she told me. "I didn't used to when I was little. I just moved the pieces. But now I always have a plan."

"What if your opponent doesn't do what you expect?"

"I try a different plan," she told me as if this was obvious. It was, of course, but I was sure there was a reason behind my questions. I didn't normally humiliate myself in front of six year olds.

"Want to play again?" I asked.

I caught myself feeling just a little too much satisfaction when I emerged victorious 25 minutes later.

12

Organizing the Design Process

"What is there to design? What happened to the idea of building a new building for manufacturing the WindSailor?" Ralph asked.

This was going to be a long meeting. It was our first official sponsor/project manager get-together, not including the one after Al quit, and I was prepared for a hard time. I had planned to educate Ralph about what would take place during the design phase. Before I answered him I thought about my own education over the last four days.

The day Al quit I had quickly informed everyone on the team and arranged to meet Sheila and Amanda in my office.

When they arrived, we talked a little about Al's sudden departure. Sheila said, "I guess seeing you in charge of this project got to him more that I thought it would."

Amanda still couldn't believe it. "Sure, we all thought he was an idiot, but was that any reason to quit?" Amanda is a very team oriented person and sometimes this gives her an unusual viewpoint.

"Since the WindSailor waits for no man, or woman," I told them, "I've made a couple of adjustments." I turned to Sheila. "You are the new designer. Congratulations. And you," I said to Amanda, "you are taking over the duties of project administrator, as well as being the user's representative."

Sheila looked happy at the new role, but Amanda didn't seem to be too thrilled. "I thought you said the user's representative role was a lot of work. How am I supposed to do both?" She was starting to sound like me.

"Don't worry," I told her. "I'll help you out."

Amanda wasn't ready to give up yet. "What about Alice?" she asked. "She doesn't have a role yet."

"Alice will have a lot to do in support of the project administrator, but to be honest, I don't think she's ready for this yet. I'm worried that she'll focus too much on the costing alone, and worry more about her accounting needs than our project needs." I smiled at Amanda in what I hoped was a friendly, supportive way. I'm sure she interpreted it differently. "See how much I admire your skills? Anyway, that's why you get the job."

"Well, in that case," Amanda said, "I've got things to do. Are we finished here?" I told her we were done, but I asked Sheila to stay behind to discuss the design.

Design Steps and the Schedule

"I think I'm starting to get a better handle on what the design phase is all about." I told Sheila my idea about the result of the design phase being an exact description of the final product. "But," I concluded, "I'm a little worried about the process of design. How soon can we get a schedule for it? And how accurate is that schedule likely to be?"

Sheila was way ahead of me. "You know, Will, I used to think that the project was the design, and the construction was just incidental." I looked at her skeptically.

"I know it sounds strange, but it's true," she assured me. "Anyway, usually the design isn't complete when the construction begins, so managing the execution has a lot to do with trying to revise the design and build at the same time."

I told her that seemed like a funny way to do it. Sheila replied, "As an engineer, most of my focus has been on the design. But I've started to change that perspective since I looked at your framework. In fact," she said, grabbing a pad of paper off my desk, "I think we can work the design process in very neatly with your consultant's framework for assignments."

On the paper she wrote:

> DESIGN (results):
>   an unmistakable description of the deliverable(s)

She said, "This pretty much sums up both of our ideas about the results of the design phase. I've just used the word *deliverables* instead of *final product*. It's a more generic word. In this assignment I'm responsible for designing more than tangible products. There are also things like training programs and information systems." I agreed that the word *deliverable* sounded better.

Just underneath that she wrote:

> DESIGN STEPS
> 1. Preliminary Design: problem solving, generation of options, feasibility analysis, proposed "best" solution
> 2. Preliminary Design Sign-off by Sponsor
> 3. Produce Detailed Design Schedule and Cost Estimate
> 4. Detailed Design Schedule and Cost Approved by Sponsor
> 5. Detailed Design
> 6. Sponsor Approves Detailed Design

She turned the pad around to me. "I'm proposing we follow this process for design. I'll explain it in a minute, but first tell me this: have you come to any conclusions about why it's hard to predict how long design takes?"

I had indeed come up with an idea. "Because every time you do a design, it's for something entirely new. That means you can't just copy an old design, you have to be creative and come up with new ideas. That creative part of the process is unpredictable."

"Right!" said Sheila. "You start with a large number of options for getting the result that you want, and you gradually eliminate them until, in the end, you have an exact picture of your particular deliverable." She paused. "The hard part to understand is that each design decision has a direct impact on all the decisions that come after it. So you don't have a very good idea about what your choices will be for the next decision until you make the current one. That also makes the whole thing hard to predict."

"I'm not sure I follow you, Sheila."

She thought for a moment. "Let me give you a little analogy. Let's imagine a baseball game. Your team is down by one run, there is one out, it's the bottom of the ninth, and there are runners on first and third. The guy coming up to the plate is pretty quick, and he's a good bunter. You're the manager. What are you going to tell him to do?"

I put myself in the position of the imaginary manager. What the hell, I thought, it's not a *real* game. "I'll go for the suicide squeeze play. I'll tell the batter to bunt the ball up the third baseline."

Sheila made a face. "You want to tie the game, your constraints are the rules of baseball, the skill of your hitter, and the fact that you have men on first and third with one out. You have a result that you want to achieve: score a run. To decide what to do, you need to do the preliminary design. What else did you consider doing?"

"To be honest, I just said the first thing that came to mind."

"You'd be surprised, Will, how often that is exactly how the preliminary design gets done. What else might you have considered before choosing the squeeze play?"

"Maybe a sacrifice fly or a hit-and-run?"

Sheila looked unimpressed. "There is only one out! What about letting your batter swing away?"

Sheila was starting to get aggressive about this sports thing. I tried to get her to move on. "So we have some options, now what?"

"You generated possible solutions, you mentally proposed what you thought was the best option, and then since you are the manager, you also completed the second step. As sponsor, you signed off the preliminary design. You aren't going to try a sacrifice fly or a hit-and-run. You're going to try a suicide squeeze. How did you come up with the options and make the decision?"

"I just picked a play that I thought would make things exciting. I didn't really weigh the options at all." Some manager, I thought.

Sheila was excited by my honesty. "That's exactly what often happens during the preliminary design, especially when you don't have a lot of time. When you were deciding what to do, information about how well your batter is able to bunt was important. Instead of making a quick assessment of him, don't you think it would have been a good idea to have a quick look through his stats? How many times has he bunted safely? What's his average against this particular pitcher?"

I was becoming a little flustered as it appeared my imaginary team was about to go down in defeat because I didn't do my research. "You didn't give me all that information. And anyway, there isn't time in a real ball game. You just have to make a choice."

"That's just it. In baseball, having to make that snap assessment is part of the game. It makes it more exciting. But do you have enough time in the real world? How much information do you collect? How long do you take to decide?"

"So this is why it's hard to predict how long design takes? Because the preliminary design requires a lot of research and a hard decision at the end." It was like talking to Martha. Sheila seemed to have all the answers.

She nodded. "That's a big part of it. Completing the preliminary design takes research and creativity, and that takes time. And if you don't do the preliminary design well, the detailed design becomes uncertain."

"So how does this help us?" I asked her. "We don't have much time, and we need to tell Ralph how long the preliminary design will be, so we can tell him how long the detailed design will take, so we can plan the execution of this damn thing!"

Sheila frowned. "That's where your designer becomes important. The project team has to rely on the skill of the designer and the feasibility analyst to generate possible options and recommend the best one."

"How do we get a good designer?"

"What do you think I am?" Sheila asked indignantly.

I backpeddled quickly. "I was thinking about assignments in general."

Sheila stared out my window. "Well, the objective statement provides the design criteria. A competent designer should be able to take those criteria and turn them into a preliminary design. The greatness of that design depends on the greatness of your designer."

This was getting a little esoteric for me. "Let me get this straight, Sheila. You're saying that the genesis step provides the groundwork necessary to do the design." She nodded in agreement. "And that the simple process you have here should allow a competent designer to produce a preliminary and then a detailed design." She nodded again. "So how long will it take?"

"I can only answer that question in two parts. The preliminary design takes a brainstorming session to generate ideas, and then the designer and the feasibility analyst have to estimate the potential benefits and costs of each so that they can recommend the best one. You also have to get the users involved to make sure their needs are met. To predict how long the whole process takes, depends on the experience of the designer, how easy it is to work with the users, and what ideas are being investigated. You can put an arbitrary time limit on it, but it takes as long as it takes."

I must have looked a little forlorn, because she said, "The good news is that once the preliminary design is complete, detailing the design is usually pretty straightforward. You can predict much more accurately how long it will take to write computer code, or draw up blue prints." I felt a little relieved. At least we might be able to predict *something*.

"How does this work for the baseball analogy?" I asked.

Sheila continued, "Once you have decided to go with the suicide squeeze, what other decisions do you need to make before execution, before the pitcher throws the ball?"

"Well," I said, taking my imagination back to the ball game, "I'd have to give the sign to everyone. I want the guy to score from third, so maybe I want him to take a big lead off the bag. On the other hand, maybe he's really fast, and I don't want to tip off the other team…"

"You're getting the idea. Our deliverable is the exact situation on the field at the moment of the pitch. Once the preliminary design has been completed, you have to make increasingly detailed decisions about exactly what the deliverable should look like. Those little decisions are easier to predict than the big decision of arriving at the preliminary design. However, your detailed design decisions will be very different if you choose a hit-and-run. And if we decide to build a whole new building to manufacture the WindSailor, our detailed design process will be very different than if we just expand some of our existing space."

This was starting to make sense. Looking back at the pad of paper, I said, "Having the sponsor's approval as we go will be key to making this work."

Sheila told me, "Especially in this case. Al told me about Ralph's preference for a new building, but that decision might be based on about as much reasoning as your decision to go for the suicide squeeze."

I felt hurt at this implied insult, but I rose above it. "Ralph has to know about the design process, so he can understand why I can't give him an ironclad schedule. At least, if he wants the best product." And then a thought popped into my head. "Most of the cost of design has to be the detailed part. Even if it is hard to predict how long it will take, generating the preliminary design shouldn't take a whole lot of money, should it?"

Sheila agreed. "That's another reason why getting the sponsor's approval of the preliminary design is a good idea. It's before a lot of money gets spent. But remember, we may run into something that we can't deal with, even during the detailed design. Finding a way around those things always takes time. The best we can do is to try and identify where in the detailed design process we might encounter delays, and keep the sponsor informed."

In the end we decided that Sheila, Amanda (the user's rep), and Stu (the feasibility analyst), would start work on the preliminary design. "How long do you think it will take?" I finally asked her.

"I thought we just decided this was unpredictable!"

"We decided it was hard to predict, not unpredictable. C'mon, I need an estimate. I have to meet with Ralph on Tuesday."

Sheila thought hard for a moment. "We've been doing work on possible plant expansions for the last year and a half, which is going to make our job a lot easier. I'm guessing at least a week to put this together. Make it two weeks, okay?"

What could I say? "You've got two weeks." I paused. "By the way, what about the ball game analogy? Once the design is complete and everyone is in position, what would be the equivalent of execution?"

"Don't you know anything about baseball?" Sheila asked. "They even call it execution! It's when the pitcher pitches the ball and everyone now has to do what they're supposed to do. The runner on third charges home, the batter bunts and takes off for first. And if you have the right resources, that is a runner who can run and a batter who can bunt, then you tie the game."

In Little League, I had always been a terrible bunter.

When is the Design Complete?

That evening found me back on Martha's porch inquiring after her health.

"Never felt better!" she declared triumphantly. "Those doctors don't know what they're talking about. It's not the pipe that's killing me, it's time!" She chuckled, took a big pull on her pipe, and blew a smoke ring in my general direction. "How's the project coming?"

I couldn't believe my ears. "Don't you mean assignment, Martha?"

"Just testing, Willie," she said, chuckling some more. "You young people are just a mite too serious."

I brought her up to date, including Al's resignation and Sheila's ideas about the design process.

"That Sheila sounds like a bright girl!" Martha said. "Sounds like you'll be much better off with her as your designer."

"So what do you think about the design process itself?" I asked. "Does it look like it will work?" I felt like a little kid who knows he has 'done good,' and wants recognition from his parents.

Martha pointed the stem of her pipe at me. "You see what a little thinking does? You don't even need my help anymore. Yessir, Willie, I like the looks of your design process. It's right up my alley."

I felt pleased, but I still had concerns. "What do I look for to help the process go smoothly?"

Martha rocked and thought for a moment. "My first suggestion is this: make sure your designer understands the logic of how things must be done before she makes up a schedule for the detailed design. That seemed to be obvious, and I said so. "We'll see about that, Willie," she said ominously.

"The second is a question. How do you know you are done describing the deliverable and are ready to plan how you are going to make it?"

"Isn't there some technical information that tells her that?" I asked.

Martha just kept smoking. "Not exactly."

I tried to think about a design I was more familiar with information systems. How did I know when a particular system was fully designed? To be honest, I wasn't really sure because we were usually implementing the system halfway through the detailed design process, and then completing the design as we went. I had to admit that I could not figure it out.

"It's a tough question," Martha said. "Mostly, it's a judgement call on the part of the designer. When she thinks there is enough detail to go ahead and plan how you would build the deliverable, then the design is complete."

"Don't you mean, when there *is* enough detail to actually build the thing, not just when the designer thinks so?"

"How do you know when there is enough detail in the design?"

I thought about my software projects. "The only way to tell is by actually doing the execution."

Martha struck like a snake. "Absolutely not!" A moment ago she had been peacefully smoking her pipe, looking like she might have been discussing the pros and cons of mulching versus bagging when cutting the lawn. Now she was sitting forward in her chair with her hands on the rocker's arms, her face red, and a little saliva bubble at the corner of her lips. I sensed this might be an important point.

"That notion has got more people into trouble than I care to remember! There is real money being spent during the execution. What if the design is not detailed enough? What if pieces are missing? Halfway into the execution isn't the time to discover that."

I mumbled something about how I supposed it wasn't and she continued on her tirade. "You make sure the design is complete by doing the execution plan! Figure out what will happen during the execution before it actually begins. Don't just start digging holes because you have a shovel in your hand!" She actually reached out and cuffed me on the back of the head.

As quickly as the storm had begun, it abated. Martha sat back in her chair. "Don't forget, the execution planning process is a test of whether the design is complete. If you come to a point in the planning process where you don't know how you would proceed because some key design decision hasn't been made, you know that your design isn't complete."

I tried to think of a simple example. Suppose you were going to build a house, and after the architect had designed it, you made an execution plan for how you were going to build it. You would decide when you would excavate for the foundation, pour the foundation, put up the dry wall, do the wiring, all that stuff. But suppose when you were planning this stuff out, you came to the task of painting the bedrooms. What if you didn't know what color they were supposed to be? Or even if they were supposed to have wood paneling instead of being painted? Maybe that was an example of an incomplete design. I related the example to Martha.

"Maybe you should have a task that has you buying the paint," Martha corrected me. "Better you should find out you don't know what color the bedroom is at that point. But yes, that would be an example of a design not being complete. Now, what might happen if a lot of these little decisions had not been made during design?"

"The execution takes longer, or costs more than you thought."

"Or both," Martha added.

"That seems pretty obvious, Martha," I told her.

She just chuckled. "Good sense is always obvious. Too bad no one pays it any notice."

Keeping the Sponsor Informed

"So you see, Ralph, this is the design process we are following." I pointed to the flip chart I had made up from Sheila's notes. "We're about halfway through the preliminary design. We're hoping to have options and recommendations for you at the end of next week."

Ralph, who had looked a little irritated when I began the explanation of the design process, was starting to look happier. I had taken him through a condensed version of what Sheila and I had discovered over the last four days, saying it as though I had always known it.

Oddly enough, Stu's idea about not treating Ralph like one of the bad guys seemed to be working. "I'm feeling more comfortable with this process," Ralph told me, "but I'm still uneasy that we don't know for certain we can be ready by June. Can't you give me at least a tentative implementation schedule at this point?"

I could appreciate how he was feeling. "I could give you one, Ralph, but I couldn't commit to it. We haven't even got the preliminary design done yet, so we don't know for sure what we'll be doing." I tried to reassure him. "We're talking to all the experts around the plant to get their very rough assessments about each option so that we're reasonably comfortable that our best option can be completed in time. But a guess now won't change how long it actually takes."

"To be honest, Will, the Hyler board is pushing me for some kind of schedule. How soon can I give them something?" Ralph was obviously trying to work with me. "If we finish the preliminary design on schedule, and we can meet with you next Friday to get your approval, we might have a design schedule for you Monday." He looked happy about that so I cautioned, "But we can't do the implementation schedule until after the detailed design is complete."

"How soon after?" he asked me.

I had no idea. I hadn't talked to Martha yet about what execution planning involved. But I tried to sound confident while I guessed. "About a week after the detailed design is approved." Ralph didn't look totally satisfied, but I wasn't going to tempt fate. "Have you got some cost tracking going?" Ralph asked.

"That was something I wanted to confirm in this meeting, Ralph. Are we going to allocate everything to this project? I mean, all of our own time as well as outside costs?" I was hoping that Hyler personnel would not be charged to the project. We could be an expensive bunch.

Ralph dashed my hopes on that one. "Everything," he told me. "We have to try and figure out the real cost of everything we do. And in-house personnel are real costs."

I had done a little preparation for this contingency. "I've set up a project number with Alice in accounting, and everyone on the team is keeping track of their time. I'll have her start accumulating our time on the project number." It meant more administrative hassle, but I could appreciate why we were doing it.

"When are you going to have this project set up on project management software?" Ralph asked.

I hedged, brilliantly. "Uh, I'm not sure."

Ralph was adamant. "I want this project run with the most modern tools we have, Will. Spend what you need to get a good package. Check with Sheila. I know Al was evaluating packages before he left."

I made a note to do that. "By the way Ralph, can we move our next Tuesday meeting to Friday? If we have the preliminary design complete, we'll need you to approve it."

That was not a problem for Ralph and we scheduled accordingly. When Ralph told me he was glad I had things under control, I didn't bother to tell him otherwise. He also said he liked these frequent meetings. Ralph was not such a bad guy when you let him know what was going on.

"Don't forget about the software," he called to me as I headed out the door. Before the project was over, I would wish that I had.

13

The User's Needs

You may find it hard to believe, but my son, Jake, is named after Jake Blues, the character John Belushi played in the movie "The Blues Brothers". I actually wanted to call him Elwood (my son, not John Belushi), after Jake's brother, because without the "Blues" last name, Jake sounded a little too much like a soap star to me. And anyway, Elwood is a much more unusual name; people remember you if your name is Elwood.

Jenny had a different opinion of the name Elwood, and after many long discussions, I gave in and we named the kid Jake. Of course now Jake is Jake, and any other name would be ridiculous. I'm holding out for Elwood to be the name of our next dog, but Jenny hasn't made any promises.

This only matters because the next week and a half sort of reminded me of the movie "The Blues Brothers." We had an objective to achieve, a short time in which to achieve it, and nothing was going to get in our way. Events moved at a frenetic pace, and we had a hell of a good time. In retrospect, developing the preliminary design was probably the most fun of the whole assignment.

While Sheila, Stu, and I worked out options and assessed them, Amanda began earning her pay as user's rep. By Thursday she came to me with a list of users that was a lot longer than I had expected.

"The union steward, what's she doing on here?" I asked. "There's no labor relations involved."

"Not quite true, Will," Amanda told me. "We're going to be hiring about 30 new people to work on the WindSailor. Our collective agreement says they have to be involved at some point. I think we should get the union onside as soon as possible. I also want them to have some input into the training programs. The people on the floor are always saying we never involve them in planning things."

"I'm sure Mark Goldman will be happy to hear about that," I said. Mark dealt with personnel issues like training, as well as labor relations issues.

Amanda said, "This assignment can't afford any delays, let alone preventable ones."

I continued down her list of users. "The city? You want to get them involved? We'll be snowed under in paperwork and bureaucracy! Can't we leave them out until later?"

Amanda looked a little exasperated. "You don't exactly have an 'abundance' mentality do you, Will? The reason we've had trouble with the city in the past is that we don't involve them until we've already decided what we want to do. Then it's very expensive for us to change our plans to meet their requirements. As a result, we resent them for doing their job."

I was still a little suspicious. "Why do we need to involve them so early?"

"In case you've forgotten, there is the little matter of access to Hyler Lake. There's also the question of sewage. We are on the municipal water system. Expanding our plant capacity by 25 or 30 percent and adding 30 employees will have some impact on our waste water."

She was starting to get on my nerves. "You've made your point. They're a user." The next name was Luigi Delgarno. I didn't bother to ask, but I assumed that since he was going to be in charge of running the process when we were finished setting it up, he should have some input.

"Why is Harry Freeman on here?" Harry Freeman was part of Alice's accounting group.

Amanda explained patiently, "We're also going to be modifying our payroll and accounting systems. Alice didn't want to be part of the user's group, so she nominated Harry. And," she said, anticipating further questions, "you'll notice Mark is on there, representing Human Resources, and Les French, from the warehouse. Revamping the plant is going to affect most areas of our existing business. Wherever people are going to be directly affected, I've tried to get representation."

I was glad it was Amanda and not me dealing with this bunch; it looked like it was going to be a lot of work. And if all those diverse interests showed up at every meeting of the project team, we'd never get anything done.

I scanned the rest of the list then handed it back to Amanda. "You may be curing me of my hesitancy to share information. This list is nothing if not comprehensive."

That wasn't quite enough for Amanda. "Will, don't forget this is a two-way street. We want their input so we can make the project work better for them, not just to pacify them."

"That's assignment, not project," I corrected her. "And yes, of course. I want to you to run all our preliminary design options past them before we recommend one to Ralph." If that didn't make me sound like a visionary, participative, focussed, quality oriented team-member, I didn't know what would.

Stu and Sheila developed alternative ways of expanding Hyler's manufacturing capacity, estimating costs, schedules, and how well they would serve our needs now and in the future. There were many variations, but the decision was really whether to construct an entirely new facility, or build onto our existing space. Each option had to be detailed enough for us to make semi-intelligent guesses about its implications. Al and Sheila's earlier work on a possible expansion of the plant meant a great deal of the leg work had already been done.

We also had some tough choices about our payroll and inventory systems. Our current payroll program couldn't handle the extra staff we would be bringing on board. In fact, the whole accounting system was old and, in my opinion, in need of replacement. And like the accounting system, our inventory control system would require significant modifications to take on the new product. The question in both cases was: modify or replace?

And so it went. Options to consider, implications to determine. All I can say is, thank goodness for Amanda. Sheila, Stu, and I had no problem coming up with what we thought were viable options, but many times our scenarios contained flaws of which we were totally unaware, and yet would have sunk the assignment had we gone ahead.

Fortunately, as soon as we had described an option, Amanda would run it by the users for their comments. We discovered, for example, that the shop floor workers were unhappy with the current trend in training. They felt that too much time was spent during the training sessions playing "games." This information had come from the union shop steward.

"When we take time off work," she had told Amanda, "We really do want to learn something. But it seems like we spend a lot of training time doing funny exercises that don't have anything to do with our jobs. We need to see a little more practical information."

This was particularly surprising for Mark Goldman, because the "games" were team-building simulations which were all the rage in personnel circles.

The biggest break we got from Amanda's work related to the city's opinion of our expansion. Based on our preliminary work, it was starting to look like Ralph's preference for a new building was going to be the best choice. We were all quite surprised when Amanda told us that the city did not approve of our plans.

"They don't like that option at all. In fact, they are pretty much opposed to us expanding," Amanda reported.

"That doesn't make sense," said Stu. "We've provide a pretty significant part of the tax base." We all felt apprehensive. Here was a stumbling block we hadn't anticipated.

"We're zoned for industrial use," Sheila said. "How can they stop us from doing what we want on our land?"

Amanda had obviously heard an earful from the city planning people. "They can deny us building permits, they can refuse to let us hook up to the municipal sewage system, and they can tie us up in bureaucracy from now until it's too late."

Stu was uncharacteristically angry, and suddenly started talking about relocating the entire plant. "If Enderby doesn't want us, maybe we should be looking elsewhere."

I sighed. "That's hardly practical Stu," I told him. "Apart from the fact that it would be horrendously expensive to move, I have a feeling that it would impact our ability to have the WindSailor to market next summer." I turned to Amanda. "Did you get a feel for why they are doing this?"

"I got more than that," she told us. "As you all know, Enderby is becoming a bedroom community of Portland. More and more people are moving out here and commuting. That means that more land out here is being zoned residential. As it turns out, the city has just approved an 80 lot subdivision for the 50 acre parcel of land behind the donut shop."

"Why does that matter to us?" asked Sheila.

Amanda continued. "The city is becoming concerned about noise pollution, air pollution, and all of those negative things associated with industry. They're worried that our new facility is going to disturb the neighbors."

"And drive property prices down," commented Stu. "I wonder how many city councilors have invested in that subdivision?"

Sheila was getting more frustrated by the minute. "We're not testing jet engines or tanks here! We're making fiberglass boards! We make less noise than a few lawn mowers!"

"Doesn't matter, Sheila," Amanda told her. "I've been over it a dozen times with them. We are industry, and the town doesn't want us putting up a brand-new building right now."

"What's the bottom line, Amanda?" I asked. "Are we dead in the water, or is there a way around it?"

We all held our breath for a minute while Amanda thought. "To be honest, I didn't get any indication there was anything we could do to get their approval." She grinned ruefully. "I guess sometimes being a little secretive helps."

"Why is that?" I asked her.

"Well, I gave the city planning people an overview of our assignment, including the part about the tight time frame. I thought they might appreciate why we want to move things quickly. They know that we can do what we want on our own land given enough time, but I think they're planning to slow us down enough so we just don't bother with the expansion at all."

Everyone looked glumly at Amanda. Stu seemed particularly depressed. "Why didn't we check into this *before* I got everything in motion?"

Sheila had been scribbling furiously. "Hang on, folks," she said, "we're not dead yet. All we have to do is provide something to the city in exchange for them not blocking our expansion. We just have to negotiate a little. From a homeowner's perspective, the city does have a point. Who wants to have a factory in their backyard?" She held up her hand as Stu was about to comment. "I know Stu, I said it myself. We aren't like what most people think of as a factory, but that doesn't matter. To your average person, a factory is a factory. It has smoke stacks that belch pollution, and it makes a lot of noise." She paused and looked around the room. "What can we offer that would be seen to make this area a nicer place to live?"

We all stared blankly at her. "Free windsurfing lessons?" Stu offered.

"No!" Sheila said with mock disgust. "What is one of the favorite recreational attractions in Enderby?"

"Hyler Lake." I said.

"Exactly! Our little lake is a very popular spot for people to go to windsurf, sail, swim, or just picnic. Technically, the lake is ours, and Hyler has agreed to maintain public access to it, but what is the main problem with the public access?"

"It runs right through the plant," I said, sure now of where she was going.

"And what do people complain most about that access?" Sheila asked.

"That fact that it runs right through the plant!" Stu said. "The city has been after us for years to build a new access off of Ascot Street. Of course we've never done it because we haven't had to."

Everyone was getting in on this. "It's been a pain in the butt for us too," Amanda said. "It means having security on site twenty-four hours a day, and we still have some vandalism and theft."

"So what are you proposing?" I asked.

"Simply this," Sheila said. "We offer to construct a new access off Ascot Street, complete with parking lot, and maybe even public washrooms, and in return, the city fast tracks all the paperwork for our expansion."

"What about the cost?" Stu asked. "We've suddenly increased our scope considerably."

"In that scenario, we don't go for the new building. It was only marginally better anyway. Instead, we go the less expensive route of expanding our existing space and building the new access. It'll still be cheaper than a new building. Then the city feels like they win two ways: they don't get a big new factory next to their subdivision, and they have a better, more convenient, access to the lake."

I still get a cold chill when I think about how close I had come to running across that "little" difficulty further along.

The Revised Objective Statement

By scrambling hard, we managed to pull a presentation together for Ralph by the following Friday. We had even received tentative approval from the city about the expansion, with the new access of course. By the time the meeting rolled around, there really was only one option, but we figured we would show Ralph all the reasoning that had gone into our final recommendation.

Sheila, Stu, and Amanda attended the meeting to help me answer questions. At the end of half an hour, I was winding things down.

"And so, Ralph, here are the specifics. We'll expand our existing manufacturing space. We will construct a new access for Hyler Lake, and we will build a new security fence between the plant and the lake. That should cut down on our security problems. In addition, we're recommending a new payroll and inventory control system. The training programs will include some new employee initiation sessions, and we're recommending some computer simulation virtual reality training for the new machine operators. We are also recommending a new supervisory seminar around performance management, for all new supervisors. If it works well, we'll expand it to include existing supervisors as well." I paused. "Once we have your approval on the preliminary design, we'll proceed with detailing it."

Ralph was busy taking notes. Finally he looked up. "How much do you estimate the recommended option will cost?"

I took a breath. Honesty had worked well so far. "Our guesstimate is now $1.6 million." Ralph scowled and I continued hurriedly. "We don't have enough detail to commit to a firm price. We will know better once we've detailed the design. But for now, that's our best guess."

"What about time frame?" Ralph asked. "Can we complete this option by June?"

"Based on our best guess, yes, we believe so. Again we'll know better when we've completed the detailed design and the execution plan."

"And how long will that be?" he asked.

I hoped we had all guessed right about this. "Three months for everything to be complete," I told him. "Some things will be done sooner, but three months should do it for everything."

"Does that $1.6 million include design costs?"

I was impressed with the question. Ralph seemed to be catching on to Martha's process. "All design costs are included in that estimate," I told him.

"Have you got a revised objective statement for me to sign?" I couldn't believe I was hearing this. As soon as we had the new estimates and the preliminary design information, I had revised the original statement. I had brought it along, thinking I would have a devil of a time getting Ralph to sign the thing again.

"Give it to me now, but I can't sign it yet." He paused. "But you can go ahead and begin to detail the design for this option." We all smiled. "I can't promise anything," he continued, "I'll have to get this increase approved by the board. But it doesn't appear we have much choice, at least if we want to proceed." He turned to Stu. "I assume you have re-run the numbers?"

Stu nodded. "I've reprojected everything based on this new cost. Our five year return on investment drops from 35 percent to 22, but it still makes sense to proceed."

"Get me a copy of the new feasibility report by this afternoon. I want to have it when I talk to Henry Stanton." Ralph then addressed all of us. "Except for the fact that you won't commit to a final cost, or a schedule, I like the way things have gone so far. But you must recognize the pressure I'm under. I'll try and continue to explain things to the board as we go, but all they want is a commitment on final cost and schedule. And Will says you'll be able to give me a final schedule for implementation a week after the detailed design is complete." We all nodded, and I hoped that I wasn't off-base with my estimate.

As we got up to leave, Ralph asked me casually if I had chosen a software package yet.

I couldn't lie because Ralph might ask me what it was. "Ah, we're just narrowing down the options. We should have our final choice by next week."

"Good!" he told me. "I'm looking forward to getting regular reports from the package. In fact, I was thinking of having it installed on my own machine here. It should save you a lot of work."

I wasn't sure I wanted Ralph playing with our plans. And anyway, what were we going to use software for? All we had needed so far was a word processor.

14

Charts, Costs, and Other Puzzles

"So what is it?" I asked.

I was sitting at my desk, staring at the page Sheila had just put in front of me. Along the top of the page was a time scale and at the left was a list of all the activities we had talked about at our detailed design planning meeting yesterday. Next to each task, placed somewhere along the time scale at the top of the page, was a solid bar. The bar length was different for each of the different tasks. It looked something like this (although this chart only shows a sample of the tasks we had on ours):

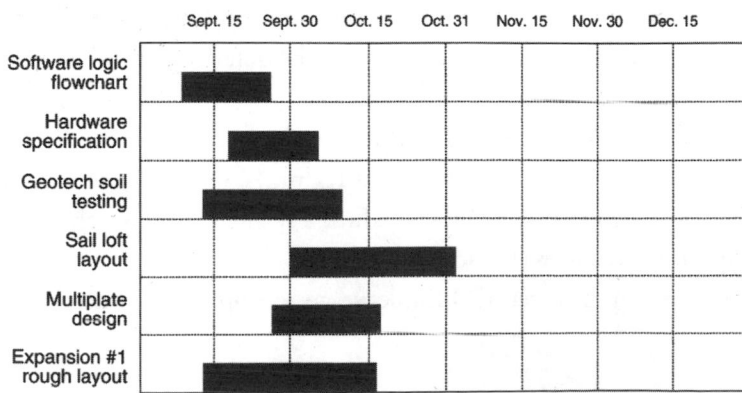

"It's a Gantt chart printout from our project management software program!" Sheila told me. When I looked blank she prodded, "You know, a Gantt chart. Otherwise known as a bar chart or a time line?"

"Of course," I said. "To be honest, I was just a little fooled by the layout. I'm much more used to seeing really messy ones that have been drawn by hand."

"Well, then, this one should look pretty good to you." She was obviously not impressed that I was not impressed. "See," she said pointing to the left-hand side of the page, "there are all of the activities in the detailed design. And those bars," she pointed to the bars, "show when each activity is scheduled to take place, and how long it is planned to be."

Ralph was going to be happy to see this: a computer generated schedule at last! Yesterday, the Monday after our meeting with him, we had had a detailed design planning meeting. Sheila, Mark, and Amanda, along with Les French, Harry Freeman, Luigi, and I had identified what we thought was a complete list of all the tasks that had to be done for the detailed design to be complete. The tasks included the design of all the building expansions (there would be three), re-laying out existing manufacturing space and layout of the new space, the training programs, the hiring process, the new payroll and accounting software, new parking lots, and the new access off of Ascot Street. That had taken the better part of the morning.

"We now have a list of tasks to complete the detailed design," I had said. "But how are we supposed to turn this into a schedule?"

"Don't worry about that, Will," Sheila told me. "I did a lot of these for Al. We'll just turn this list into a Gantt chart schedule. I can have that for you by tomorrow morning." Sure enough, here she was with the schedule in hand. "How long is the detailed design going to take?" I asked her.

"Good news, Will, it looks like about nine weeks."

That was good news—we had told Ralph 12 weeks. "Are contingencies built into that schedule?" I didn't want to commit anything to Ralph that wasn't well padded.

"You were in the meeting. I think we've accounted for everything."

"Stretch everything out a little so that it takes 12 weeks, in case something does go wrong. And what about the cost?" After listing all the tasks, we had figured out what resources were required to do each task. Sheila was supposed to go away and, based on the total time required of each resource, estimate a cost.

"About $125,000, if we include all the Hyler resources." I was still getting used to the idea that we had to charge our own people's time to this project. It sure made it a lot more expensive. "That's more than we originally estimated," I told Sheila. "Where is the extra cost coming from?"

She looked defensive. "There isn't any extra cost. When we figured out all the tasks and resources, it just came out higher than I guessed at."

"I'm not trying to blame you," I said. "I was just wondering why the first guess was low."

"The first guess was just that, a guess. When we figured everything out in detail we just had a lot better information."

"Fair enough. We're about $35,000 higher now on our cost estimate for the detailed design. Do you think we should get Ralph's approval?"

"We didn't actually tell him how much the detailed design was going to cost, we just gave him the total project cost. Personally, I wouldn't bother him. An extra $35,000 out of $1.6 million isn't much. Who knows, maybe the execution will cost less than we're estimating." That jibed with my feelings. Why bother the sponsor over a mere $35,000? "Ralph told me he'll have the extra $600,000 in overall cost approved by tomorrow. Why don't you start getting all our ducks in a row so we can begin the detailed design as soon as I have the signed objective statement."

I looked again at the Gantt chart printout. "Let's get back to this project management software for a minute. Ralph has been bugging, but I've been putting off making a decision. Is this package going to be our choice?"

"Well, actually, Al and I had been evaluating project management software packages for about a month before he left. I just bought the one I liked the most. But you can go through all the demo packages if you like."

I just smiled. "Sheila, I'm extremely happy that you've already made the choice." She looked relieved. "I wouldn't have known where to begin."

I asked her to leave the Gantt chart behind as I wanted to show it to my consultant. She left after I told her that I would contact her as soon as I heard from Ralph.

I sat back down at my desk and looked over the bar chart. Give me a nice simple tool any day over some complicated, mathematical chart that was confusing to read and hard to decipher. I expected our Gantt chart was going to impress our "consultant".

Coping with Delays

"You didn't listen to my advice did you, Willie?" She blew a smoke ring my way and rocked back in her chair. Hadn't I been listening to all of her advice? I tried to recall something she had told me that I'd decided to ignore. I came up blank.

"Martha, as far as I know, I've been doing everything you've told me to do. And," I added, partly as proof of this statement, and partly to try and soften the old girl up with a little praise, "things have been going extremely well because of it."

Martha took her pipe out of her mouth. With the stem she tapped the Gantt chart that lay on the little table between us. "This is your schedule for your detailed design, is it?" I nodded. "Let me ask you a question then, Willie. What happens to your finish date if this task takes two weeks longer than you expect?" She was pointing to a task labeled "Geotechnical assessment of base stability".

I pretended to cough to give myself time to think. The task was supposed to start in three days and run for a week, but what was it? I tried to remember our detailed design planning session. I seemed to recall that Sheila said something about the soil under one of the building expansions being a little unstable because it was close to the edge of the lake. Yes, that was it! And in order to design the foundation properly, there had to be some kind of soil assessment. I felt relieved. I hated looking stupid in front of Martha. My relief was short lived however. I knew what the task was, but how was I supposed to figure out how a delay in this one task would affect the finish date of the whole detailed design? I casually took my handkerchief out of my pocket to blow my nose and cover my confusion.

"You don't have a clue do you, Willie?" Martha asked me smugly.

"This is complicated engineering stuff, Martha," I told her. "I'm sure my designer could tell you." I hoped it was true.

"I'm not so sure, Willie. But how about this task?" She was pointing to one of the software design steps, something I did know about. "What happens to the finish date if this task is delayed two weeks?"

I hemmed and hawed for a few seconds, but couldn't come up with an answer. "There is an important lesson here, Willie, one that will be vital to understand when it comes time to plan the execution. I won't tell you what it is just yet though; I think you'll appreciate it more if you knock your head against it a few times. I will repeat my hint though: don't ignore the logic!"

The old bat wouldn't say anything more about it even when I pestered her. To make matters worse, she started having one of her coughing fits.

Making Adjustments

Tuesday night turned out to be a bad night all round. After I helped Natalie put Martha to bed, I returned home to find that Jake had some kind of coughing sickness of his own. The poor little guy couldn't stop hacking, and we ended up running the hot water in the shower to fill the bathroom up with steam, then Jenny and I took turns sitting with him in the steam bath until he finally fell asleep at about 3 a.m.

By 6:15 a.m. the next morning I was 2,000 feet below the surface of the ocean, collecting specimens of deep-sea plant life for the U.S. Oceanographic Survey. Suddenly an electronic beeper went off in my diving helmet, and I knew that I had less than six minutes of oxygen remaining. As I struggled for the surface I faced a terrible dilemma: come up too quickly and die from the rapid decompression, or drown on the ocean floor. I was paralyzed until a voice spoke to me. It said, "Turn the damn alarm off!"

By the time I got to work I was starting to wonder if maybe I shouldn't have just taken the day off. Luckily, there was a pick-me-up waiting for me. It was the revised objective statement, signed by Ralph. He had attached a note asking me to bring him the schedule for the detailed design as soon as I had it.

I ended up leaving work at about three in the afternoon, but it was still a very productive day. I met with Ralph to present him with Sheila's Gantt chart (after she had lengthened the schedule to 12 weeks), and let him know that he could expect regular reports coming out of our newly selected software package. On the spur of the moment, and against my better judgement, I also told him about the increase in the detailed design cost. To my surprise, he was fairly reasonable. I guess I had prepared him well for the uncertainty about guessing at design in the early stages. We decided not to revise the objective statement yet, as it was a small increase relative to the overall budget, most of which was still guess.

I also got Sheila started on executing the detailed design. She told me she was contracting for some of the engineering design, and that she was putting Hans Schmidt, one of my people in Information Systems, in charge of the software work, with my permission of course. Hans would be reporting directly to her for work on the assignment. It all sounded good to me so I told her to charge ahead.

I arranged for Amanda, as the project administrator, to take over the software from Sheila. We installed a copy of the program on her computer, and she started to read through the instruction manual. Sheila agreed to help out until Amanda was comfortable. I was confident it wouldn't be long. Coming from my department, she has to learn software quickly.

In the end, I forgot all about what Martha had told me the night before.

15

More Problems with Schedules

Four weeks later I was hovering over Amanda's workstation, trying to find out what was wrong with our project management software.

"Explain this to me again please, Amanda," I asked.

"Like I told you, Will, I've been keeping our plan up-to-date on a daily basis. Every time one of our detailed design activities starts, I put the actual start date into the software, and every time something finishes, I put that in too. I want to make sure we stay right on top of this schedule."

"That's good," I told her. "I really do appreciate your efforts. But why is this a problem?"

She continued, "That part isn't the problem. The problem happened here," She pointed to the screen, which was displaying the Gantt chart schedule. Her finger was on one of the software design tasks. "Hans told me that he is having this task done by a local consultant because we don't have the expertise. It just finished now."

I looked at the screen, and for the first time noticed that there were two bars for every task listed. The top one appeared to be the planned start, finish, and duration of the task, and I guessed that the bottom one would represent how long the task actually took. The task she was pointing to should have finished two weeks ago. "What does this do to our completion date for finishing the detailed design?" I asked, trying not to sound panicky.

"That's where the problem is!" Amanda told me triumphantly. "I don't know! When I put in the actual finish date, the finish date for the whole schedule didn't change. That's when I suspected we might have trouble. I went back and looked at the other design tasks that have finished. Look here and tell me what you see."

As I ran my finger down the screen, there were several instances where the second bar (the actual duration) for a task was a little longer than the first (the planned time). "It looks like most of our tasks are taking a little longer than planned," I told her.

"Bingo! That should have changed our scheduled finish date. And that's why I think that we must have a problem with this software. It doesn't seem to be calculating correctly. If it was, we'd have a new finish date with all these delayed tasks."

I stepped back from the machine and tried to put my information system's hat on top of my project manager's hat. It didn't fit very well. "Let's call Sheila in. Maybe there's something about the software we don't understand." Five minutes later she was looking over Amanda's other shoulder. She couldn't figure it out either. Since we weren't about to check the programming code, I decided we had better eliminate human error first. I asked Sheila to describe what she had done when putting the design tasks into the package.

"I input the names of all the tasks, then assigned the resources we had planned to have on this project, and I included their hourly costs. After that, I went down the list of tasks and scheduled each one based on my best guess of when it would take place."

"So then how did you come up with a finish date for the detailed design?" I asked.

"I got it from the finish date of the last task that I had scheduled."

It appeared to make sense, but I was not yet ready to believe that the software was the problem. Suddenly, my conversation with Martha from four weeks ago started to come back to me, and I could feel little beads of cold sweat forming on my back. I turned to Sheila. "What would be the impact on the finish date if this task,"—I pointed to the one that had touched off this whole discussion—"finishes two weeks late?"

Sheila looked hard at the screen and chewed her bottom lip. Finally she said, "I can work it out, but I think it changes the finish date by about three weeks."

"Three weeks?" I asked, just a little too loudly. "We don't have three weeks! I told Ralph 12 weeks for the whole thing."

Sheila gave me an exasperated look. "Don't forget, Will, I padded the schedule by three weeks, like you asked. Besides," she added, "you said it yourself, the design is a little unpredictable. Don't worry, we'll get it done."

"That's not what's bothering me. It's the fact that we've been taken by surprise. And this software doesn't seem to be telling us what the new finish date is. Any ideas?"

Sheila continued to stare at the screen. "I guess I'll have to go through each task and give it a new start and finish date to bring it up to date."

Amanda wasn't sure. "I don't know, Sheila. There should be a better way."

I thought there should be a better way too, but Sheila assured us that this was how it was done on other projects, and that she would spend more time helping Amanda update the status.

"How long before you can give me a estimate of the new finish date?" I asked.

"About an hour," Sheila told me.

As I went back to my office, I couldn't help but wonder if maybe we weren't doing something wrong. An hour to recalculate the schedule! Not exactly lightning quick. Martha understood that we would run into problems at this point. I would have happily suffered a lung full of smoke rings to find an answer, but she was off visiting her son in New Jersey. She had a habit of going East in the fall to see the leaves change color. Personally I figured there couldn't be too many trees left in New Jersey, but never having been anywhere except Newark, I suppose I was in no position to judge.

Completing the Design

The next eight weeks were some of the most stressful of my life. Not because things went wrong; they didn't. And not because things were out of control; they weren't. It was just a feeling that I was unprepared for surprises. Every time something changed—and believe me there were a lot of little changes—I had to yank Sheila off whatever she was doing to help Amanda figure out the new finish date.

I tried to get Sheila to show Amanda or myself how to recalculate the schedule, but she had so much information in her head that we couldn't get the hang of it. All the while I cursed Martha for being so cryptic and for letting me learn whatever lesson I was supposed to be learning the hard way.

Halloween came and Jenny and I took the kids around the neighborhood so that they could collect candy for me. It is tough to be a parent at that time of year, but I believe the sacrifice is worth it in the long run. Consequently, I was at the health club riding a Lifecycle to rid myself of the caloric sacrifices I had made for my children when one of the women who worked at the front desk approached me.

"Mr. Campbell?" she asked.

"Yes," I said, turning my head a little too suddenly and spraying her with sweat. You would think people who work in health clubs would be used to this kind of thing, but maybe she was new.

"There's a phone call for you at the front desk," she told me as she grabbed a towel and wiped frantically at her face. I guess "Wagon Wheels" don't smell so great when they come out of your pores.

I hopped off the bike and suddenly had a tight knot in my stomach. I was hoping it was some kind of home emergency and not my project.

"I've got some good news and some bad news." It was Amanda.

"Can't you come up with something original?" I asked her. "If I had a nickel for every time I've heard that cliché," I trailed off, waiting for her to get the joke. After a few seconds of silence, I said, "It's a good thing I don't pay you for your sense of humor."

"That was a joke?" she asked, a little too innocently.

"Just tell me the good news and the bad news," I said impatiently. "I'm in the middle of my workout."

"I just came out of a meeting of the Enderby City Council, and they've changed their minds."

This made the tight little knot in my stomach even tighter. "Changed their minds?" I echoed.

As the user's representative, Amanda had done an excellent job in getting the city engineers to agree to our proposed changes. In fact, we were proceeding with the detailed design on the assumption that the city approved of our plans.

The one hitch was that the whole thing had to be passed by the city council. The engineers who worked at the city assured us that whatever they recommended, the councillors would agree to, and that the meeting was just a rubber stamping process. Apparently this was not the case.

"Remember Bud MacDonald?" Amanda asked. I didn't. "He's one of the councillors, and he is also a retired civil engineer. He used to work for the Water Department in Portland." I slumped against the wall. "Anyway, he considers himself to be an expert on water and sewage systems, and he wants us to build a small on-site waste treatment facility, to process all of our water before it reaches the municipal system."

When I hear phrases like, "on-site waste treatment facility," I see dollar signs floating before my eyes. I slumped even harder against the wall I was already slumping against. "You said you had some good news," I said weakly.

"The good news is that we have the town's approval as long as we do the on-site waste treatment!" Amanda actually sounded excited. I decided to calm her down a little.

"Amanda, do you have any idea what this on-site treatment facility is going to cost? And how much time it will add to our schedule?"

"I don't know about the schedule," she said, "but I talked to Bud after the meeting—"

"Bud?" I interjected. "This guy is the enemy, and you're on a first name basis?"

Amanda gave an exasperated huff. "He's not the enemy, Will. He's simply doing his job. And anyway, as user's rep, I want to be on friendly terms with the users." She was right, of course. "Bud told me about a self-contained treatment system that he figured would be large enough for our plant and that would meet the city's requirements."

"How much?"

"About $50,000. And according to Bud, about four and a half weeks to do all the design and preparation work for the installation."

I had mixed feelings about this information. When I heard $50,000, I was relieved. I had been imagining a price about five times that. But the four and a half weeks for the design brought back my out-of-control feeling. I had no idea how much time that was going to add to our schedule.

"I guess we'll have to get together with Sheila first thing tomorrow morning and figure out the impact on our design schedule. And then I'll see Ralph about the increased cost." I paused for a minute. It was important to give credit where credit was due. "And by the way, Amanda, you're doing an excellent job as user's rep. It's a good thing that one of us gets along well with the city."

When I hung up the phone, the guy at the front desk tossed me a towel. "What's this for?" I asked him.

"To wipe off the wall where you were slumping. Otherwise we'll have to charge you for repainting."

It's a good thing Halloween only comes once a year.

For reasons that Sheila was never able to explain adequately, the extra time for design work on the on-site sewage treatment system did not extend the completion date of the design process. I thought it would, but she said, "It has to do with how all the tasks interrelate. It's hard to explain."

When things are "hard to explain", I tend to feel nervous. In the heat of the moment, I had forgotten what I had learned from Martha: Any plan that is unexplainable is not really a plan.

In the end, I didn't exactly get burned by our poor plan, just a little singed. Our detailed design work was completed on the 18th of December, just over 13 weeks from when we started. This was only one week longer than our estimate, and Ralph was pleased.

I had a different feeling. It was as if I had been dozing at the wheel of my car and awakened to find that the car had driven off the road and then come to a stop at the edge of a cliff, all of its own accord. Until the end of the eighth week, Sheila had been predicting we would be finished in nine weeks. Then she discovered a few things that needed doing, and some of those things had tasks that came before them that hadn't been done yet. When we finished only a week late, I felt we had been saved from disaster by luck more than anything else, and I vowed not to let that happen during the execution. I vowed to visit Martha a little more frequently.

Fortunately, that would be much simpler now with the approach of Christmas. The old girl had been having such a good time watching leaves change in New Jersey that she wouldn't be arriving back into town until December 22. Things pretty much shut down at Hyler over the Christmas week, so I figured this would give me plenty of time to find out about Execution Planning from Martha.

Part Four

Execution Planning

16

Tasks

It was Christmas Eve, and we were all over at Jenny's parents' place for our annual Eggnog Fest and Present Opening Celebration. Jenny's sister and her family were down from Seattle and all the kids were playing noisily together on the livingroom floor, never straying far from the presents under the tree. This was going to be Jake's first Christmas as a conscious participant (he was almost three now), and we were all looking forward to it.

"So go on, Willie," Martha prodded me. "Finish up your story." I had been giving her a summary of what had happened during the detailed design process.

"In the end, we managed to wrap it up in a little over 13 weeks, despite, or maybe because of, all my worrying." The relief of having finished, along with the eggnog, was making me a little sentimental. "Everything is done. All the design for the training, new systems, org charts, blueprints, the works! We had a team meeting. Everyone was there, including Ralph and Stu. Leslie brought some champagne and we all toasted when Ralph signed off on the detailed design. It was a great way to break for Christmas."

Ralph had pulled me aside to ask when I would have the schedule for the execution complete. Some of the board members were still impatient and needed to be assured. "I've promised it to Ralph for the first week in January."

"Did you figure out what was causing you to feel uneasy during the detailed design?" Leave it to Martha not to savor the success.

It was Christmas, so I figured I might as well be truthful. "To be honest, no. I just had this feeling that we weren't understanding the implications of the changes."

Martha shook her head and said, "Take a little stroll with me out to the porch."

"It's about thirty-five degrees out there!" I protested. Thirty-five degrees isn't that cold when you've grown up with east coast winters, but it's amazing how quickly you get soft when you move to a warmer climate. Besides, I knew the only reason Martha wanted to go outside was so she could smoke her pipe. Pipe smoking did not justify freezing, at least not in my book.

"Don't be a wimp, Willie," she told me as she tottered toward the front door. "A little brisk weather is invigorating. How do you think I got to be eighty-nine?"

Bad luck? I got up from my nice warm chair, helped Martha on with her coat, took mine off the coat rack, and followed her onto the porch. It was actually quite a nice night. Darfield is a small enough burg that the city lights don't out-shine the stars, and this Christmas Eve was clear and beautiful. As I looked up at the sky, savoring the clear night, a smoke ring drifted past my nose, like a warning shot across the bow: Martha's way of saying it was time to get down to serious business.

"I'm a little disappointed, Willie," she told me. "I thought you might have worked out your problem before I got back." She blew another smoke ring in my general direction.

"Believe me, I tried," I told her.

As always, Martha was subtle. "Willie, it is obvious." She was overusing my nickname, so it had to be something she thought was particularly simple. "Tell me again why you felt out of control."

Of course nothing came to me, so I resigned myself to having Martha lead me through the maze. "Every time something changed, I had to get my designer to tell me what it meant to the schedule. And even she didn't always know what changes meant. She thought we were going to finish in nine weeks right up until the end, and then she discovered she forgot about something, and it took us an extra four weeks to complete. Luckily, I had padded the schedule a little, and the sponsor was still quite happy."

Martha jumped on me. "If you depend on luck to get you through assignments, you're in for a lot of pain," she said crossly. "Whenever you don't understand something as fundamental as how all the activities fit together it's time to think hard about the problem, not just press on and hope it doesn't matter!"

Easy for her to say. She didn't have Ralph breathing down her neck. "Don't you think adding a little slack to the schedule is a good idea?"

Martha took her pipe out of her mouth, then hawked and spat off the porch. Sometimes the old girl can be a real charmer. "Understanding the fundamentals of the situation is paramount, Willie. Padding schedules that are based on guesses is not a useful way to make up for this lack of understanding. You got lucky this time. Do you want to try and be lucky during the execution as well?"

I decided to sit on my ego. "No," I told her. "Just explain to me how I can understand the fundamentals."

She took a long pull on her pipe and held the smoke in her lungs until I thought she would explode. Finally she let it out. "Let's think about the execution plan. If you had to draw me a picture of the assignment as it sits right now, what would it look like?" She looked over at me expectantly.

"That's a bizarre question. What would it look like? I have no idea."

"Humor me, Willie. Just draw it." She handed me a pad of paper.

I took the pad and stared at it. Draw what the assignment looks like? Suddenly, I was inspired. I drew something that looked like this:

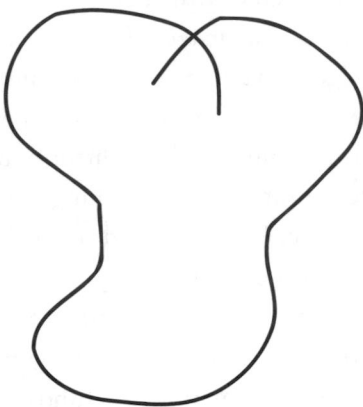

Martha said, "Explain it."

"This big blob represents all of the work that has to get done during the execution: all the construction, all the hiring, all the training, everything. There are probably several hundred tasks that have to get done, and right now they are all jumbled up in this big blob of work."

It must have been the answer Martha was expecting because she went right on with her questions. "Why is it one big blob instead of as a bunch of little blobs? Say, one for each task?"

"Because you wanted me to draw the project as I see it now. We haven't figured out what all the individual tasks are yet. Right now it's just one big mess, and by next Monday we have to have a schedule and a cost for this blob."

Martha surprised me by saying, "Very good, Will. You have a pretty accurate picture about where you stand. Or," she added, "where you sit." She chuckled, although I have no idea why she found this funny. "How will you take this big blob and put a cost on it and figure out how long it will take?"

I described what we had done for the detailed design plan. "We'll break the blob into individual tasks, assign resources to them, and then schedule them." I wasn't confident about this since it hadn't quite worked the last time.

"And what will you need to know about each task?" Martha asked.

I rattled off the information we had collected last time. "What the task is, how long it takes, and the person or people that are going to do it."

Martha's questions continued. "And how will you use this information to schedule this task along with all the others?"

I opened my mouth to answer and then closed it again when I realized that I didn't know. "I'm not really clear on that part Martha. In fact, that's where we had most of our problems with the detailed design."

"I'll give you a hint, Willie," she said. "You're missing one piece of information about each task."

"Missing information? What else is there to know?"

"Don't you remember?" Without waiting for me to answer, she went on. "Let me give you a better hint."

A Simple Set of Tasks

She picked up the pad of paper and tore off my blob. "Tell me, Willie, what do you have to do in the morning to get ready for work? And give me your pencil." She reached out her hand.

I handed her the pencil and looked at her questioningly. "To get ready for work?"

"Trust me, simple things make complicated truths simple."

I played along. "Well, I get out of bed, I shave, I shower, I get dressed, eat breakfast and read the paper, and then drive to work." I paused and then said, "I also help Jenny get the kids up, maybe change a diaper, help make the kids some breakfast, have some mashed bananas spilled on my tie, change my tie, notice there are also bananas on my shirt, change my shirt—"

"Enough, Willie! Let's keep it simple." She turned the paper toward me. On it was written:

Shower
Shave
Get out of bed
Eat breakfast
Get dressed
Drive to work
Read the paper

"Is this what you do in the morning?" she asked me. I allowed as how it was close enough. She continued, "Let's suppose that we are doing an execution plan for what you do in the morning. We have a list of the activities, what do we need after that?"

"We need to know who is going to do each task, which will be me, and we need to estimate how long each one takes."

"Let's do just that," Martha said.

When we were done, the list looked like this:

	Who?	How Long?
Shower	WC	8 min
Shave	WC	7 min
Get out of bed	WC	10 min
Eat breakfast	WC	25 min
Get dressed	WC	8 min
Drive to work	WC	15 min
Read the paper	WC	25 min

"It takes you ten minutes to get out of bed in the morning?" Martha asked me, rather overdoing the incredulity, in my opinion.

"I like to listen to the news on the radio," I said defensively.

Martha again turned the pad toward me. "Would you say that this is an adequate execution plan for your morning routine?"

"You don't have them in the right order, but otherwise that just about says it all."

"You've just hit on something, Willie," Martha told me, and

looked at me as if she should be seeing a light bulb over my head.

"What's the big deal? You just rearrange them until they make sense, right?"

Instead of answering my question, Martha handed me the pad and started to load up her pipe again. "Put the sequence in the column to the right-hand side." When I was done, the page looked like this:

	Who?	How Long?	Sequence
Shower	WC	8 min	3
Shave	WC	7 min	2
Get out of bed	WC	10 min	1
Eat breakfast	WC	25 min	5
Get dressed	WC	8 min	4
Drive to work	WC	15 min	7
Read the paper	WC	25 min	6

I handed the pad of paper back to Martha. She glanced at it and said, "Does it take you 1 hour and 38 minutes from the time you wake up until the time you arrive at work?"

"No," I said, "It takes more like an hour or an hour and ten minutes. Why?"

She tapped the page with the list of activities. "That's what it says here."

I took the pad back and added up the times. Sure enough, the total was 98 minutes. I stared at the list for a second, unsure where the extra time was coming from. "I see the problem, Martha. I read the paper and eat breakfast at the same time." I handed the list back to her. We were getting into a serious game of hot potato with that list.

Martha looked at the list again. "This still tells me that it takes you 1 hour and 38 minutes." She handed it back. "Do you understand what this list is telling us now—and it's not doing a very good job— that it didn't tell us a few minutes ago?"

"Sure," I said, "the order of the tasks." Suddenly, a light bulb did go on. "Wait a minute, Martha! This is where the problems started for us in the detailed design! We had a list of activities, but we weren't really sure of the sequence. At least none of us except Sheila. Come to think of it, Sheila wasn't really sure of the sequence since she kept making mistakes. And that meant we couldn't tell what would happen if certain tasks took longer."

Martha looked pleased. "Be a little more precise, Will. In fact, the information you need to collect about each activity or task is: what it is, how long it will take, who will do it, and *how it relates to all the other activities*. Not exactly the sequence, but how all the activities fit in with each other."

She paused and puffed on her pipe. When she continued, she was quite somber. "Will, this is something that I don't expect you to grasp right away. Not because you are stupid—this isn't that complicated—but because it's an idea that eludes most people. The idea is this: the logic of how the activities must go together to produce the desired outcome of your assignment *determines* the schedule of your project, not the other way around. Most people are guilty of what I call Gantt chart thinking. When it comes time to plan the execution, they figure out what the tasks are, how long each should take, and then simply decide when they ought to take place using nothing more than a calendar and a sketchy, intuitive grasp of sequence and what the interdependence among tasks may be. The result is a schedule that is not based on simple cause-and-effect logic." She looked at me and smiled. "Like what you handed me back in October."

Grasping the Logic

Martha continued on. "When you are figuring out how to execute an assignment, you're not creating something new. You are simply revealing the underlying structure of the best way for things to go together. Let me give you an example, Will. The human race did not invent the elements on the periodic table. They were always around, waiting to be discovered." She turned and pointed her pipe stem at me. "It is the same with projects. Your job during the execution planning stage is to reveal the logic of the best approach. And that logic is what determines how long your project will take. A must be done before B, and B before C and D. If you want to do things otherwise and compromise the logic, your chances of achieving your desired outcome decrease dramatically."

"Can you give me an actual example of when the logic was ignored?"

She glared at me a little and puffed her pipe. "You can give me one from your detailed design process."

As soon as she said it, I knew she was right. Sheila had scheduled the work of laying out the new manufacturing and warehousing space independently of the design of the new inventory control system. It happened that both were supposed to be done in the eighth week. What Sheila forgot was that the inventory control system was going to identify specific inventory locations throughout the plant. So we were missing information about where and how big the various storage and holding spaces would be throughout the plant, and that delayed the completion of the plant layout. We had tried to do two activities in parallel when they had to be done in sequence. I related the story to Martha.

"You would be amazed, Will, at how often a schedule is derived not from the logic but from someone's guess. Of course, the fact that it was a guess shows up during the execution. Unfortunately, that is when it's most expensive to correct."

I was not all that amazed. Logic must have been in the back of my mind, as I'm sure it was in Sheila's mind, but I never thought of it as *determining* the schedule.

I looked at the pad of paper. "I have one problem with all of this Martha. It looks like it gets really complicated. Even our detailed design plan had about 50 tasks. How do you show all of the logic on this list without boggling your mind?"

"Let's just say," she said, "a picture is worth a thousand lists."

Santa was kind to everyone that Christmas. Jake and Sarah both got toys too numerous to mention. Jenny gave her mother a beautiful handknitted sweater, and Jenny got a pair of excellent quality leather hiking boots in return. Fred got the handyman's usual assortment of tools for his workshop, and his gifts to everyone else had been hand-made in said workshop: a toy box for Sarah, a rocking horse for Jake, a spice rack for Jenny, and some lovely lawn animals for Natalie. I've always wanted wooden skunks on my lawn. Maybe Fred will make me some one day. I can only hope.

We all chipped in and bought Martha a brand new pipe and a large supply of her favorite tobacco. Pipe related paraphernalia have become a regular Christmas gift for Martha. Thank God she smokes that pipe or we wouldn't have a clue what to get her.

And as for me, I got the usual assortment of things the young father and son-in-law receives: new ties, socks, underwear, and after-shave. But I got something even more valuable from Martha. Something that I couldn't wait to try out back at work the following week.

17

A Dependency Chart

I had the feeling that my personal popularity was at an all-time low with my project team. I could tell this by the expressions on people's faces as they sat around the conference table and stared into their coffee. It was the 28th of December, the Thursday after Christmas, and not even our now traditional box of donut holes was making a dent in the black cloud that was hanging near the ceiling of the conference room. I had been expecting a little bad feeling but, as the Californians like to say, the reality of all the negative energy was getting me down. Generally, only keeners and losers (with nothing else to do) show up at work during the Christmas break. Right now I wasn't sure whether my project team considered me a keener or a loser.

Mark Goldman started us off with a rousing round of, "How long do you think we'll be here?"

I began with my team building address. "I apologize for breaking in on your holidays but Ralph wants to see an execution plan right after New Year's, so this is our only time to get it done. As to your question Mark, I expect we'll be here until about 2:00." Everyone groaned. "We may be finished sooner, but I want to get our first cut at our execution plan done today."

At this point Sheila piped up with, "I've loaded the project management software onto my laptop, Will. To save time, we could plan the execution right on the computer." This brought a lot of positive nods. People often think things will go faster if there is a computer involved.

Fortunately, Martha had warned me about this. "Actually, Sheila, I want to approach this execution plan in a slightly different way. I've been in touch with the project consultant again and she suggested some new ideas that I want to try."

"She?" asked Luigi. "I thought the consultant was a he." Trust Luigi to pick up on that.

"Sorry, he. I've been having a little too much eggnog and it's rattled my brain. Anyway, I want to try his process." I turned to Sheila and Amanda. "He's also solved our computer software problem." Of course, after Martha had explained things, it was obvious that the software wasn't a problem, but I thought I would save that until later.

I walked over to the wall of the conference room. Like a lot of companies, we have a four-by-eight foot erasable white board hanging on one wall of the room. Martha told me that I would need all the space I could get.

"We are going to use something called a dependency chart to help us develop our execution plan." I had thought hard about how I could briefly summarize Martha's ideas for them. "Our assignment now looks like this." On the white board I drew a reasonable facsimile of the blob I had drawn for Martha. "The design phase is complete, and there are now a whole bunch of activities that need to be done so that we can be ready to produce the WindSailor."

"To create the execution plan we need to break this huge blob of stuff into discrete tasks that we can assign resources to, cost, schedule, track, and eventually accomplish." With a marker I drew lines across my blob, sectioning it into little pieces to illustrate how the blob was just a bunch of activities.

"Our job today is to identify each of those activities. But to do our execution plan properly, we need to know four things about each one of these bits of work: what it is, how long it takes, who or what is needed to do it, and how it relates to all of the other tasks." I stopped and wrote on the white board:

> Description
> Duration
> Resource(s)
> Interdependency

"The first three are fairly easy to figure out. We did it effectively during the planning of the detailed design. The fourth item—how each task relates to all of the other tasks—is not so easy.

"If there were only a few activities, we could just number them from one to the end. Our project is more complicated, and most of the activities will not be sequential. We'll have several tasks going on at any one time, and we will need to be aware of all sorts of complicated relationships among them."

"So instead of writing all that information down in a big table or a list, we're going to draw a picture." I took a three-by-four inch pad of sticky notes and held it up to the group. "We're going to put each task on one of these yellow stickies—name, resource, and duration." On the top sticky I wrote out a sample task:

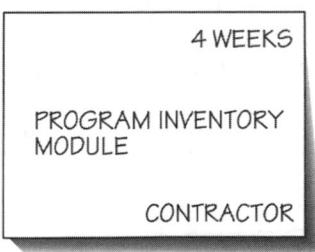

"As you all know, some of our tasks will be related to upgrading our information systems. For a sample, I've picked one of those." I read out the information on the sticker. "Once we identify a task, we stick it on the white board." I stuck the sticker in the middle of the board.

"Now comes the tricky part: How does this task relate to all the other tasks?" On another sticky note I wrote:

I read the information to everyone. "Anyone care to guess how this new task relates to the one we already have up here?"

"It comes after it," Amanda volunteered.

"Exactly," I said. "It comes right after it. So now I stick this task to the right of the first task." I did this and then uncapped my marker. "And now the final thing we need to do is show that the two of them are related. How we are going to do that?"

"With a line," Sheila said and without waiting for me to draw it continued. "Now I understand the problem with the software! It was missing information. I had all of those lines inside my head, and not in the computer." It was the same revelation I had talking with Martha, but I didn't want to spend time on it now.

"Precisely, Sheila." I drew an arrow from the first task to the second. "This picture is called a dependency chart. It shows how all the

activities depend on each other. According to my consultant, it's the simplest, best way to plan the execution."

Leslie said, "This makes a lot of sense. It's big and visual so that all of us can get involved in the planning. I was expecting we would all be hunched over a computer screen."

I tried to capitalize on what Leslie said by touting a couple of other advantages that Martha had pointed out. "The fact that we use these sticky notes and the white board means that we have a lot more flexibility during the planning. Any time we don't like what we've got, we can move the stickers somewhere else, erase the lines, and draw new ones. And according to Marth—"—I had to catch myself —"Martin, the consultant, once the dependency chart is finished, the whole thing is ready for computer input."

Only Mark and Alice were looking at me with that have-you-been-drinking? look. You know the one I mean. Martha warned me to confront the skeptics early, otherwise the planning process could fall apart so, I said, "Mark, Alice, something seems to be bothering you two."

They looked at each other and then Mark spoke up. "Isn't that dependency chart thing going to be awfully complicated? I mean, wouldn't it be simpler to draw a bar chart or work from a list?"

"That's what I was thinking too, Will," Alice chimed in. "I may not have gotten along with Al Burton very well, but he was a project management expert and his project plans were always simple bar charts, very easy to understand. How come he didn't use something this complicated?"

I said, "Let me ask you both two questions. Is it important to know the logic of how the tasks relate?" I waited for their answer. Finally they nodded their heads grudgingly. "Okay, we need to know the logic. Now, how can we best keep track of the logic?"

After a pause Mark said, "I see what you're getting at. Even a small project has lots of links. Keeping them inside your head would be a disaster, and anyway you would have no way of showing anybody else how the tasks fit together."

Alice still wasn't convinced. "But it's still going to be complicated."

"Only if you try to conceive the whole thing at once. At the individual task level, it will really be quite simple. You'll be able to look at one of these stickers, see what the task is, how long it takes, who is going to do it (or what), then look at the lines to see how it relates to other tasks."

"I guess I'll go along with it for now," Alice said finally. "We'll see what it looks like at the end."

Sheila said, "Don't forget, Alice, once we have all this information, we can produce a bar chart like you would normally see. Only this time it will be based on something other than guesses."

Changing Perspective

I was anxious to get going so I continued, "Martin also suggested two other things. The first was that we plan the project from the end to the beginning. He called this *objective driven logic.*"

Luigi asked, "Why do that? It's only going to make the whole thing confusing."

"According to the consultant, looking at it from the point of view of 'It's finished, now how did we get here?' will give us a different perspective on the plan, and help us create a better one." I gave them Martha's example verbatim. "Think of a jigsaw puzzle. When you dump it out of the box onto the table, the first thing you do is look at the picture on the box so you can see where you are supposed to end up."

Alice said, "Well, if your consultant does it that way we should probably give it a try."

It always amazes me how people accept so-called expert opinions. In the future, whenever I have a good idea, I'll just claim some consultant suggested it.

"What was the second thing, Will?" Mark asked, getting us back on track.

"We are going to put this plan on a time scale." I turned to the white board and began drawing vertical lines on it, about a sticker width apart. "The space between each pair of lines will represent one week. When we're done, we'll have a rough idea of how long this should take." When I finished putting the time scale up I turned around to face the group.

"I'm afraid there are two more things that I need to introduce about dependency charts: float and the critical path." This brought looks of dismay to most faces. "Does this have to do with PERT or one of those fancy mathematical models?" Sheila asked.

"Relax. There is no math involved. And the two ideas are very simple. Let me illustrate. As I picked up the pad of sticky notes I said a silent prayer that I would be able to make this look as simple as I had when I was practicing last night. "I'm going to plan a very simple project to illustrate how dependency charts work, and also show you float and the critical path. I won't even use real task names, just letters of the alphabet. Now, what is the last task in any project?"

Everyone had a blank expression. "Remember team, we're using objective driven logic. That means starting from the end and working backwards." The room was alive with excitement. When no one said anything, I decided to help them out. I wrote on one of the stickers and then said, "The last task in any project is this," I held up the sticker so that they could see it.

"This is a milestone. It has a zero time duration, it just marks the event of the end of the project." I stuck it on the planning board.

"The next-to-last task in the alphabet project is task Z. Task Z takes two weeks." I wrote this on the sticker. "Task Z must be done before the end of the project, and we have to show its duration on the time scale. It's really quite simple." I counted back two weeks from the End Project sticker and put the Z sticker down. Then I drew an arrow from the task Z sticker to the End Project sticker.

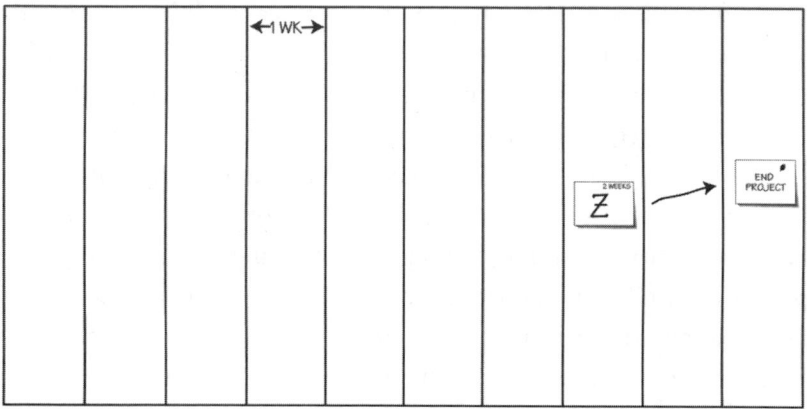

"I changed my mind," Mark said. "This is too simple. We'll be here forever if we have to do this for the whole project!"

"Give me a chance, Mark." I tried to hurry things along. "Now I just ask myself a simple question. What has to be the case before we can start task Z? And as I answer that question for each task, we generate more tasks, we stick them on the chart, and very quickly—" here I looked pointedly at Mark, "we generate a plan. In this case, task M must be completed before task Z starts." I had been going to use most of the alphabet for the demonstration, but I decided to cut to the chase.

"Task M takes three weeks." I wrote the name and duration on the sticker. On the board I counted back three weeks, put up the sticker, and drew an arrow from M to Z.

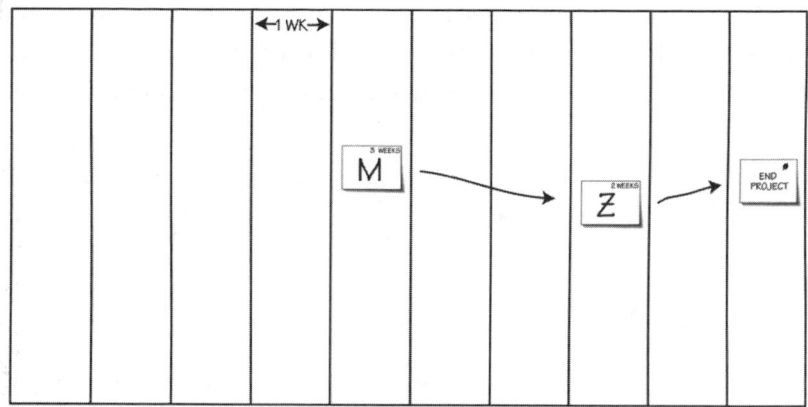

"Is there anything else that comes before task Z?" I asked the group. I had intended it to be a rhetorical question but Alice said, "I have feeling you are going to tell us."

"You bet. Task L also comes before task Z. Task L takes two weeks." I wrote this on a sticker, put it on the board, and drew an arrow.

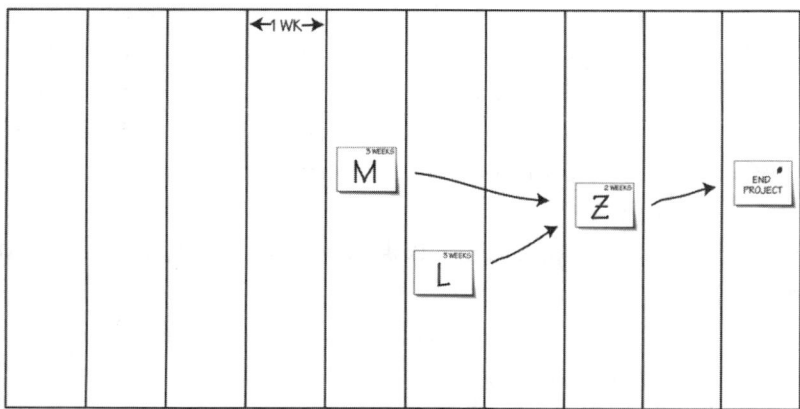

"If you can hang on for three more tasks, all will be revealed. So now we have to pick either L or M and work backwards from there. Any preferences?" They say effective speakers try to get their audience to participate, but my team behaved like witnesses at a New York crime scene; they did not want to get involved.

"Well, then, let's pick task L. What has to be the case before we can do task L? As it turns out, we need to have completed task D. Task D takes two weeks." I wrote this on a sticker and put it on the board.

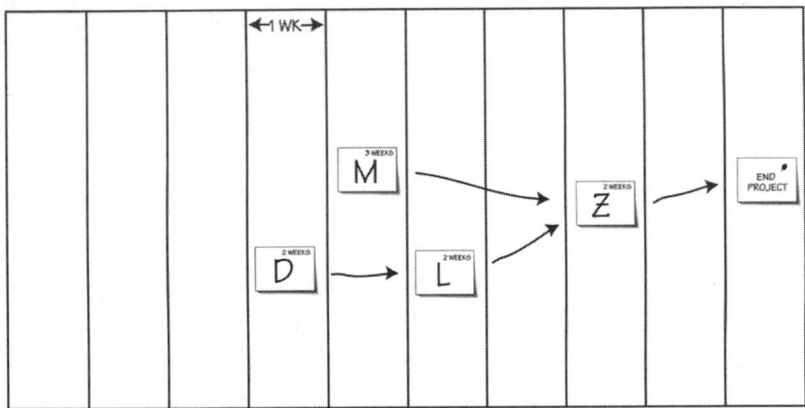

"Anything else before task L? In this case, no. So let's move on to task M. What has to be done before task M?" I paused to let the team ponder this question. Before they went to sleep, I gave them the answer. "Before task M can start, task D must be done. In other words, task L has the same predecessor as task M. That's okay, it happens all the time in projects. But we do have one problem. Can anybody see what it is?"

Amanda finally spoke up. "Task D isn't finished before task M starts."

"Exactly!" I said enthusiastically. "Because we're doing this on a time scale, we can see right away that D has to start a whole week earlier than we thought so that it can be done before M. Luckily, we are using an erasable board and movable tasks. I'll just move D and erase the line, then connect it to M."

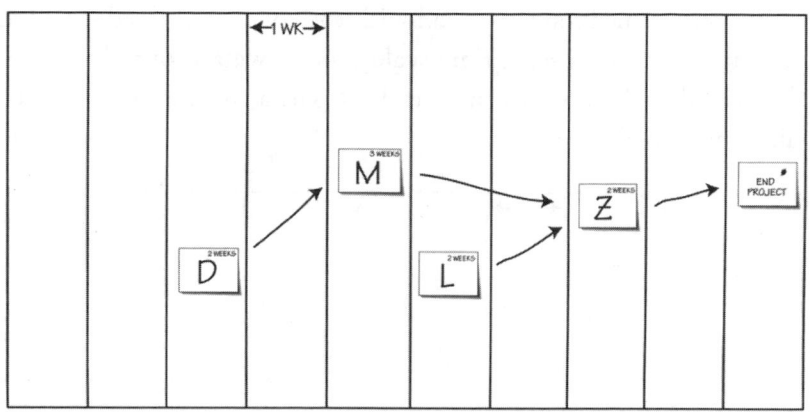

A Float

"What's our problem now, though?"

Mark pointed it out. "D used to be linked to L, but now it isn't."

"Good!" I said. "And that is where the concept of float comes into play. It is the slack time between when D ends and L begins. We show it on the dependency chart with a squiggly line." I drew in the dependency relationship on the board and now the picture looked like this:

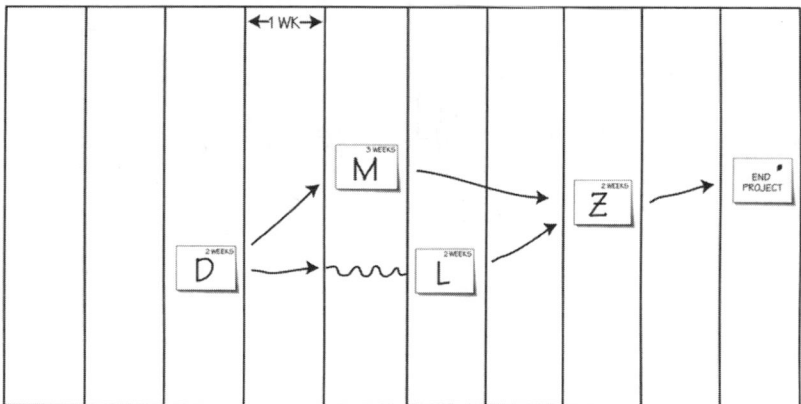

No one seemed too impressed with the concept of float; it was so obvious when you used a time scale. "Next we ask ourselves what has to be done before we can do task D. The answer is task A which takes three weeks."

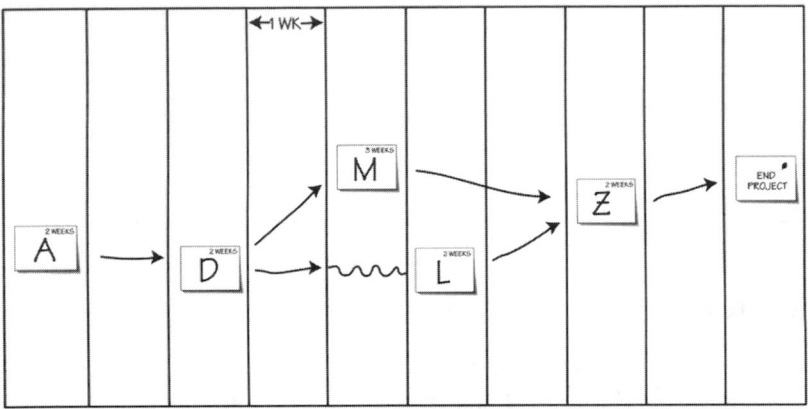

"Finally, we ask ourselves what comes before A. The answer in this case is, The start. This is another milestone, and like the end, every project has one." I stuck a start sticker up to complete the plan.

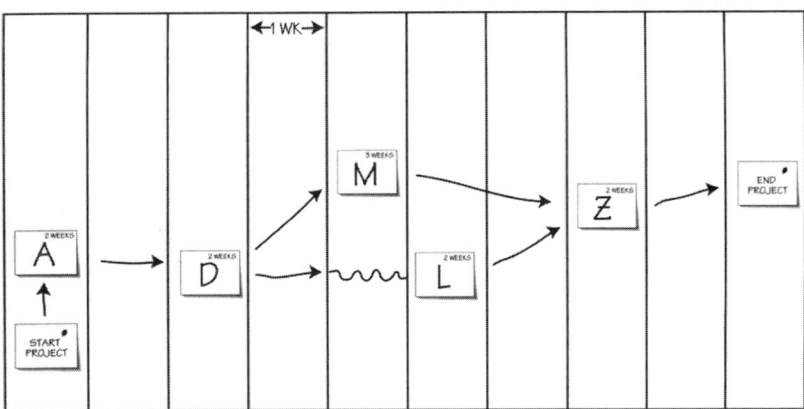

I surveyed the group. They were no longer openly hostile. "What about the critical path?" Alice asked.

"Let me make one more point about float first," I said. "Let me ask you a question about the float around task L. What happens to the finish of this project if task L is delayed by one week?"

Everyone stared at the board for a moment until Mark said the obvious. "The finish is delayed by one week, assuming nothing else changes."

"Exactly. Now what happens to the end of the project if task D is delayed one week?"

Luigi spoke without thinking first. "The float gets used up and the project finish doesn't get delayed."

Sheila was quick to correct him. "Look at it again, Luigi. If task D gets delayed, it delays M, which delays Z, which delays the finish."

"So what's the point of having the float?" Alice asked. Finally, the audience was going where I wanted them to.

"That is a good question, Alice. As much as possible we want the float to come after the particular task or activity with which it is associated. That way, if something goes wrong, we have the float as a cushion. So," I turned to the board, "if we just move the task, without changing the logic, we can make use of the float." I picked up task L, erased the line, put task L in its new position, and redrew the line.

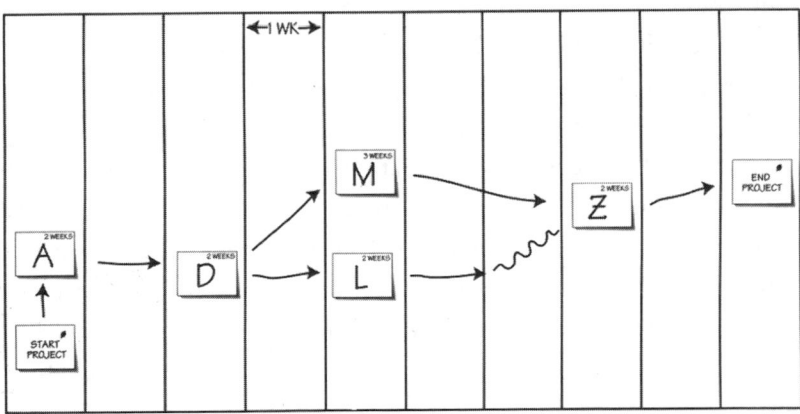

"That is all we need to know about float," I said.

The Critical Path

"The last thing is the critical path. The critical path is simply the path with the least amount of float." I looked around the table. "In this project there are two paths: start-A-D-M-Z-end, and start-A-D-L-Z-end. Which one is critical? Call out the letters of the path as I go and I'll make it with a double line." When we were done the chart looked like this:

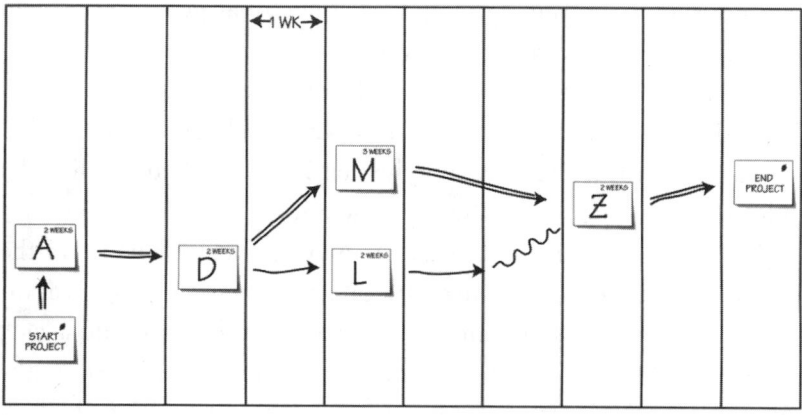

"As you can see, finding the critical path is simple—no math required. You just find the path with the least amount of float. Now why would we care about the critical path?"

"Because it's critical?" Mark said, only half joking.

Sheila said, "Because it's the path that takes the longest to complete."

"Exactly! Does everyone see that? It's the longest path and therefore it determines how long the project will be." Everyone nodded their head in agreement, making me feel that perhaps I had oversimplified things. In fact, as Martha had explained, there was no simplification involved. There wasn't any complication involved either. I had just shown my team everything we needed to understand about putting the execution plan together.

When is a Task a Task?

Alice raised her hand like she was still in school. "I have a question. What's the difference between a task and an activity? And how big is a task anyway? I mean, what kind of ground rules are there for defining one? Is it cost? Or duration?"

Thank heavens I had asked Martha the same questions. "A task and an activity are the same thing; a bit of work that we have to get done. As for how big to make one, what kind of ground rules should we use?"

Everyone jumped in. "Use a dollar limit." "How about a time of between one week and one month?" "A combination of duration and cost." Finally someone said something useful. "Why not define each one in as much detail as we need to be able to control it." We all turned to Amanda, the profferer of this advice. "What I mean is, putting some arbitrary dollar figure or time limit on what makes a task is pointless. Why don't we just make tasks based on our own judgement?"

That was exactly the answer I was looking for. Martha had harangued me for some time about this one. "That is what the consultant recommends. In his words we should define the tasks in a way that makes sense. For example, a task like 'Hire and train workers' is way too broad to be of much help to us in managing this thing. But 'Tie shoelaces' is probably a little too detailed." As Martha put it, we were supposed to make the task as small as the dependency logic demands.

We spent a little more time talking about tasks, critical paths, dependency charts, and the depleted state of the donut holes. Finally, we got down to doing our execution plan.

"Okay, let's start at the end and work backwards." I pointed to the End project sticky note that I had put on the far right-hand side of the whiteboard, then I paused and surveyed the room in what I hoped was a commanding manner. "So what do we do just before the end?"

No one said anything. I couldn't blame them, I felt the same way. This planning-backwards stuff was going to be hard work. "How about a task called "Hand over facility to Production?" I wrote this on a yellow sticky and put it up on the board, drawing a line from it to the End task.

"That should be the last thing we do, for sure," said Luigi. This interested him, of course, since he was in charge of production.

"What about 'Move Retail Facilities'?" suggested Alice. "As you know, the design calls for the retail store to be moved to the other end of the plant so it's next to the new public access."

"One of the last things we do is the paving for parking at the new retail outlet," chimed in Mark.

I was frantically writing on yellow stickies as tasks were named. Finally I said, "I can't keep up. Look, let's work on one thing at a time. If you think of a task that doesn't relate to whatever we're currently working on, just jot it down and bring it up at the right time. It's important for us to focus on the same part of the project plan and not get scattered."

As Complicated as it Needs to Be

Four hours later we stood back to admire our work. Mark said, "It looks like a spaghetti dinner." Luigi disagreed. "Too messy," he said.

We had over 80 tasks with all their logic relationships stuck up on the board on the time scale. As well, we had identified the resources required to perform each task. It was a significant amount of information in one place. Best of all, at least in my eyes, our time scale was telling me that we would be finished during the third week of June— barring surprises of course.

"Ralph isn't going to like it," warned Alice.

I reacted a little defensively. "Why wouldn't he like it? That's our execution plan right there, all the information we need to know. What's not to like?"

"All I'm saying, Will, is that it looks complicated. Ralph doesn't like complicated things, and neither does the Hyler board."

I should have paid more attention to Alice's comments, but I was too high on our plan. "Does everyone agree that we now have a real handle on this execution plan?" Everyone nodded vigorously. "Is there any information on this plan we could do without?"

Sheila was adamant. "Absolutely not, Will! Everything is there in one place. Sure it looks complicated, but once we put it into the software we'll be able to clean it up."

I felt satisfied. "There you go, then. This is only as complicated as it needs to be. I expect that both Ralph and the board will appreciate that." I turned to Amanda. "I'm meeting with Ralph January 3 at 2 p.m. Can you get this into the software before then?" She nodded. "Great! I'll see you all back here after New Year's!"

I felt good about the day. We had put together the best plan I had ever seen, and we had done it without much disagreement. With Martha's simple rules, the plan had almost built itself. Looking back, the only thing I would have done differently would have been to listen more closely to what Alice had to say.

18

Finding and Fixing Mistakes

"Daddy, why is your smile turned down all the time?"

Jake was really starting to talk a lot now but how do you explain to your almost three year old kid that your damn execution plan is screwed up because all the resources are overloaded, the cost is about $1 million more than your original estimate, and the thing won't finish until November, five months late? I guess the answer is, you don't.

"Daddy has a lot on his mind right now, Jake, and sometimes all of this thinking makes my head hurt."

"Play with me and it makes your head better, Daddy."

"Okay, Jake, what do you want to play with?"

"My blocks!" What else. His great grandmother, none other than Martha herself, had given him blocks for Christmas and ever since he has used all of his spare time—something you have a lot of when you're three—building things with those blocks.

As Jake laid his blocks out on the floor and got ready to create another skyscraper, I pondered my situation and prepared to assist him. Okay, I admit, the blocks are fun. It had only been a day since the high of completing our execution plan. At that point, everything had seemed under control.

But this morning, Amanda and I had come into work to put the plan into the project management software. We had both planned on spending no more than a couple of hours getting it set up. At six in the evening our difficulties still weren't resolved.

The problem was that the program was telling us things we didn't want to hear. It was telling us things we didn't even believe to be true. For example, according to the program the project would finish November 18. But because we had done the plan on a time scale, we could see that it finished in June. We had also done a rough estimate of the costs from our plan on the white board (we could do this because we had identified all of the resources for the tasks), and came up with $1.4 million. We were all comfortable with that for a rough cut. But the software was telling us $2.5 million would be required!

It had taken us longer than expected to input the plan from the white board, and by 6 p.m., after spending two fruitless hours trying to find out why we and the software were in disagreement, we had decided to call it a night.

"No bump, Daddy!" Jake said, startling me out of my reverie. I had knocked my elbow against one of his just constructed spires.

"Sorry, son." The little guy was getting pretty testy about his blocks. When I was a kid I had always thought knocking things down was the best part.

I watched Jake trying to stack single blocks as high as he could. He was getting frustrated because after the sixth block, the whole thing kept tumbling down. Try as he might, he couldn't make it stand. I could see his problem: he was not stacking the blocks square on top of each other. The second block was slightly off kilter with the first one, and the third block was only slightly off as well, and when the two mistakes were added together, it spelled collapse by block number five or six. Just to prove my theory, and to show Jake how a master builder does things, I stacked a pile ten blocks high.

Jake looked closely at my pile. He examined it up and down, and then he went back to his own pile. This time, he placed the blocks very carefully, and he was able to get up to eight blocks before he accidentally knocked the whole thing over when he turned to pick up another block. This started him crying and since it was 8:30, I took him upstairs to bed.

Later, as I sat playing with the blocks all on my own, I started to think about our software problems. And, because I like analogies, I started thinking about the process of inputting as if it were like stacking blocks. It was done piece by piece, each bit of information depending on the rest. If mistakes were made stacking the blocks, the whole thing fell apart. If mistakes were made inputting the data from the white board, it seemed to me the result would be the same.

When I thought about it, we hadn't really been all that systematic about entering the project. We didn't set out to make mistakes, but we were in a bit of a hurry. And when we tried to find mistakes, we spent more time staring at our original plan and the computer screen than we did looking for simple inputting mistakes. We had been looking for a big error in planning, or some obvious calculation error the program was making. It never occurred to us that the problem might be much simpler.

The next morning, I found that I was right. We had made no fewer than 17 different mistakes in entering the plan into the computer. We had about six of the logic links entered incorrectly as well as several task durations that were wrong. In one case we had accidentally typed "4m" (four months) instead of "4d" (four days). When Amanda corrected those errors our schedule suddenly had a finish date of June 23.

Our costs had decreased significantly as well, but I checked all that information just to be on the safe side. Sure enough, we had the hourly rates wrong for several resources. I resolved that in the future, I would be much more careful about getting the data from the planning board into the computer.

When we had completed all my corrections, I was confident that the software was giving us correct data. I was also confident that I didn't want to be at work any longer. It was Saturday after all.

Delivering What's Wanted

"But where's your Gantt chart? And your work breakdown structure?" Ralph sat back in his chair.

I had just presented our plan to him, proudly displaying our dependency chart. Apparently Ralph was not as impressed as I had been. "Well, uh," I mumbled.

Ralph turned to Stu, who was sitting beside him watching the presentation. "I thought I made it clear that I wanted a Gantt chart and a work breakdown structure!" He turned back to me and glared. "Is it too much to ask to give me the plan in the format I requested?"

"Um, I, ah."

Ralph stood up. "There is a board meeting next Monday in Portland. I will be expected to provide an update on this project, which means that by Friday I want to see a Gantt chart schedule and a detailed work breakdown structure. Is that clear enough?"

I nodded, not trusting myself to say anything intelligent, and Ralph strode angrily out of the boardroom.

"Nice going, sport," Stu said as he put his feet up on the conference table. "You really showed him that you know what you're doing."

"But, Stu, why does he want to see a Gantt chart, or a work breakdown structure? All the information is right here!" I tapped the dependency chart that was taped to the wall. "This is the basic tool for the execution plan." Besides, I thought, I'm not even sure what a work breakdown structure is.

Stu took his feet off the table. "To be honest, Will, I'm impressed with the planning work that you've done so far. And that dependency chart looks complicated at first, but it really does provide a good picture of the project. There's only one problem."

"What's that?" I asked.

"I'm not the sponsor. Ralph is, and if he wants to see his plans a certain way, then you've got to present them that way."

"Even if his way is wrong?" I retorted.

"Even if his way is wrong. Look, Will, Ralph pays the bills. He's like your customer, and he is always right. If you feel a dependency chart is the tool that you need to use to manage the execution then, great, use it. But if Ralph wants to see things in a different way, then you have to accommodate that too." He leaned back in the chair. "Right and wrong may not be good words to use here. If your dependency chart is such a great tool, it should be no problem to produce whatever arrangement of information that Ralph wants."

Stu was making sense. Ralph had a different perspective. And it didn't matter to him that Gantt chart thinking had gotten us into trouble during the detailed design. I was supposed to take care of the details and give him his information in a format he could understand.

"There is one other thing that you should know, Will. Mantec's stock is down on Wall Street and there is talk of changes within the organization. That means that Ralph's future is a little unsure, and it's making him nervous."

I was not impressed. "So he takes it out on me and this project?"

"Yes, he does. That's the reality of having to work with other people. Their problems become your problems." He stood up to leave. "Ralph is not against you, he just needs to have some things his way. I think he has done his job as sponsor pretty effectively so far. Get him his Gantt charts and work structures, or whatever, and he'll continue to do a good job."

Thirty minutes later, I was with Sheila in Amanda's office, briefing them on the meeting. "The upshot is, we have to produce a Gantt chart and a work breakdown structure, whatever that is, for Ralph before Friday so that he can be ready for Monday's board meeting."

"And so that we can get going on the execution," added Amanda. "Don't forget why we're doing this. We need Ralph's approval to continue."

"Yes, of course," I said testily. She was right, but it was easy to get caught up in doing things to keep your sponsor happy, and forget about why you were really there. "I guess Ralph isn't going to trust us about dependency charts, and that means lots more work for us, reporting in the way that he likes."

I guess I was overdoing the martyr stuff because Sheila said, "Give me a break, Will. It isn't going to be much work at all. Our dependency chart has all of the information, so any variation, like a Gantt chart, is easy to produce. Here," she punched a couple of keys on Amanda's computer and pointed at the screen.

"It looks like a Gantt chart," I said.

"It is. It gets created automatically when we enter all of the project data. We just have to print it out."

"Why didn't you tell me we had one? How come you didn't print it out for my presentation?"

"As you may recall, Will, you specifically did not want anything but the dependency chart. I asked you, but you told me,"—her mimicry made my voice sound pompous—"'the dependency chart has all of the information, why would I want anything else?'"

I felt sheepish. "So the software already produces it? There's no extra work?"

"The Gantt chart is there already. The work breakdown structure will be a little more work."

"How much?" I groaned. Inwardly, my martyr side was happy. I wanted Ralph's request to turn into some extra work, otherwise how could I resent him for it?

"About fifteen minutes."

My martyr hopes were dashed. "Fifteen minutes? Maybe you should start by telling me exactly what a work breakdown structure is."

Rearranging the Information

Sheila was happy to comply. "Until we did our dependency chart, I used to think of work breakdown structures as a project planning tool. Now I would just call them alternative ways of arranging project information."

"That's a bit cryptic, isn't it?" Amanda asked.

Sheila tapped the computer screen. "All we have here is a big database of information about the project, task names, durations, resources, links, and so on. The dependency chart is the best tool we've got to help assemble those data, but once it's together, we can arrange it any way we want. That's where the software comes in very handy. It allows us to produce new and different arrangements at a moment's notice. A Gantt chart is an example of a new arrangement of data. It shows the task, the duration, and the schedule, but it doesn't show the logic. For it to be correct of course, it has to be based on the logic."

"So the work breakdown structure is just another arrangement of the data?" I asked hopefully.

"Not exactly," Sheila said. "The work breakdown structure has to do with grouping the tasks into different categories."

"For example?" Amanda prompted.

"Well, the most common choices are to group the tasks based on the functional area within the organization, by scope items, or by the phase of the project."

"For example?" I said.

"In this project, we might group the tasks under the headings of Systems, Human Resources, Operations, and Construction. Under Systems we would put tasks like program new inventory control module, and debug accounting module. Under Human Resources we would put all the training and hiring activities. Operations would get tasks like the equipment purchase, warehouse racking, and so on." She scribbled on a pad of paper, and when she was done, this is what her picture looked like:

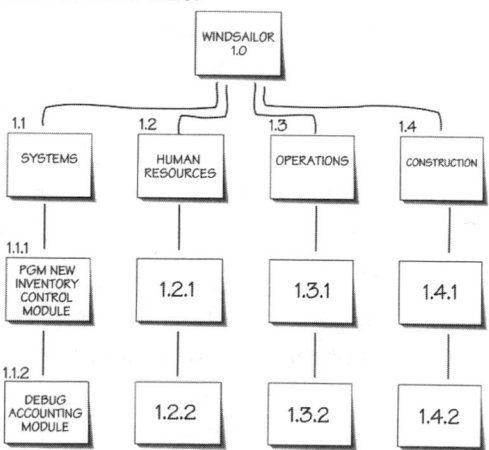

"It usually comes with its own hierarchical numbering system to identify the tasks," Sheila told us, explaining the numbers she had jotted on the chart.

"Great," I said. "We have an organizational hierarchy for the project, but why would we want this? It doesn't seem to have any practical application for managing the execution."

"I didn't invent them, Will. In fact they mostly get used for costing purposes, so different departments can budget for project work. All we have to do is decide how we're going to group the tasks, input that new information to the software, and it will print a chart."

"Okay," I said without too much enthusiasm. "But how do we group the tasks?"

Amanda is always full of good ideas. "Why don't we just use a structure that Ralph has seen before?"

Sheila said, "Al had a generic one that he wanted to make standard throughout Hyler. I think it was based on functional group. I'll check his office."

We spent the next hour and a half forcing our project into that mold. I was beginning to accept that the idea of satisfying Ralph, so long as it didn't greatly interfere with doing the assignment within the constraints of the objective statement, might not be such a bad thing after all.

Signing Off the Execution Plan

At the Friday meeting, Ralph was in a better mood, and I gave him what he wanted. I also got accidental vindication of my belief in dependency charts. As we were staring at the Gantt chart, Ralph asked, "How come the training on the new forklifts takes place so much earlier than all the other new equipment training?" We were purchasing special forklifts to transport the WindSailor hulls from the manufacturing space to the warehouse for curing.

"We'll be using existing staff to operate the new forklifts, but we'll use new hires to run most of the other new equipment," I told him.

"Well, in that case, why don't we buy them now so the staff can get used to them?"

"Because we need to have the new warehouse space constructed and laid out before we purchase the forklifts, otherwise we'll have no place to conduct the training, or to store them. There's no point spending the money before we can use the equipment."

"What about storing them in the new dinghy manufacturing space?"

"We won't have access. Our old access road is being torn out to accommodate the other warehouse expansion."

Ralph had another question. "How do you keep all of this information in your head?"

Unable to resist, I pointed to the dependency chart next to me. "I don't need to remember. It's all here."

Ralph looked from the dependency chart to the Gantt chart and back again. His only comment was, "The Gantt chart sure is easier to read."

I resisted saying anything.

Ralph was very pleased to sign off on our execution plan. The extra costs didn't bother him, I assume because we had showed him where they came from, but he did have a question about costs.

"Why aren't your contingency costs the standard ten percent of the total project costs?"

"We did it a little differently this time, Ralph. We tried to think of what might go wrong, and then we planned how we would respond to it. We then attached a cost to our response plan and estimated how likely we thought it was that we would have this particular thing go wrong. After that, we multiplied the probability times the cost for each contingency and added them all up. We felt that would give us a better estimate of contingencies."

It had been Martha's idea to cost contingencies this way, but I wasn't completely in agreement, especially since our contingency costs were 16 percent of the total execution cost instead of the usual ten percent. However, given her record so far, I was willing to go along with it.

Ralph was not. "Drop your contingency costs to ten percent and I'll sign off." I didn't fight hard for Martha's idea, although as I thought about it later, it really made better sense. More than an arbitrary ten percent.

Just as he was leaving the conference room, Ralph said, "By the way, Will, I want you at the board meeting Monday. I think the board should see your presentation of the project."

Stu chuckled. "You're getting to be a popular guy."

Part Five

Execution

19

Altering Plans

Our neighbors, Harlan and Eileen Kilbrew, were strange. Little things made me feel this way, like the way he had his hair cut (as if he went to a soup bowl dealer, not a barber shop), the way she always fixed her glasses with tape instead of glue, the fact that they gave their dog Chunky, a golden retriever, haircuts. I assume they didn't use the same bowl.

My worst fears were confirmed when I noticed the two of them coming out of the video store. There, under Harlan's arm, was the classic Tim Conway video, "Dorf on Golf." I had serious reservations about living next door to anyone who watches "Dorf on Golf" of their own free will.

I was getting out of my car when I noticed them. I had stopped at the video store to pick up something for the kids to watch with the babysitter while Jenny and I went out to dinner. The project execution phase had been under way for three weeks and things had been going well; I thought a little celebrating was in order.

I tried to hide in a casual manner but Eileen saw me crouched down behind my car. "Hi, Will! Did you drop something?" She rushed over to help me while I frantically took my keys out of my pocket and pretended to pick them up. "Oh, hi Eileen, Harlan. Didn't see you. I was just looking for my keys." I held them up. "Here they are! Don't trouble yourself." I was trying to head her off before she got close but it was too late. Eileen caught her foot on the bumper of the car and fell heavily into me. The frame of her glasses crunched against the bridge of my nose and the tape gave way.

"Honey bun," she called to Harlan, "I've dropped my glasses. Come help Will find them." I reached down and picked them up. She must have been really nearsighted because each lens felt as if it weighed about a pound.

"Thanks, Will," she said, pulling a roll of scotch tape out of her pocket and fixing her frame on the spot. This kind of thing happened to her a lot.

"So, Will, I hear you've got a little competition," Harlan said while Eileen taped.

"Harlan, would you mind not leaning on my car with your keys in your hand?"

"Oh, sorry," he said. "It's just a little scratch. It'll buff right out."

I've often wondered how they get by in the world. What's really bizarre is that Harlan and Eileen own the sporting goods store in Enderby. Somehow they do okay, although I've never met any couple less athletic than those two. Of course their store sells windsurfers, aluminum fishing boats, and day sailers, so Harlan feels he and I have some kind of special bond.

"Like I was saying, Will, your competition is getting the jump on you. I just got a flyer from California Water Sports introducing their new product. It's called the WindWalker. It's kind of like a cross between a windsurfer and a small sailboat."

For the first time since I had met him, I was interested in what Harlan was saying. "You just got this flyer in the mail?" I asked, a cold sweat forming on the small of my back.

"Yessir," Harlan. He was obviously pleased that someone cared about what he had to say. "Just this morning. They're claiming they'll have it ready for us dealers by July. I'll tell ya, it looks like they've got a real winner. It should be a lot easier to sail than a windsurfer, yet much more portable than a sailboat. I mean, you can put it on the roof of your car. And the best part is, once they sail the WindWalker for a year or two—"

"—the customer will move up to either a new windsurfer or a day sailor." I finished the sentence. I couldn't believe what I was hearing. Our projections were based on having at least a year's head-start on the competition. Something twigged in my head. "Harlan, what did you say the name of the company was?"

"California Water Sports, from San Francisco. They make the Wind Ripper and the Weasel and the..." Harlan proceeded to give me a list of every product that the company made, but I stopped listening very quickly. I knew the reason we had lost our head start. Al Burton.

The next day Ralph, Stu, Carrie Starblanket (the vice-president of Marketing), and I gathered in the conference room. Carrie had done some digging via sales reps and agents and had come up with a synopsis of what had transpired at California Water Sports. I felt as if we were at a military briefing after an ambush.

"As you all know," Carrie told us, "California Water Sports is a smaller company, with about $30 million in sales. Just after Al left us to join them, Darnell Holdings purchased the company. Is everyone familiar with Darnell? No? Darnell is similar to Mantec. It has holdings in shipping, trucking, and manufacturing. We're not sure why they acquired California Water Sports, but they certainly appear ready to provide all the support it needs.

"Soon after Al arrived in San Francisco, and soon after the company was purchased by Darnell, CWS did a product development tour of Europe. They spent some time in Eastern Europe, and apparently hooked up with a company in Odessa that has this new product, very similar to our WindSailor. With Darnell's backing, CWS has purchased the rights to manufacture and sell it in North America. With the money that their new parent company is providing, CWS plans to have the product available to dealers by July. And here's the kicker: they're planning to outspend us on advertising by about two to one!"

"What about patent violation?" Stu asked. "Any chance they could be infringing on the WindSailor?"

Carrie shook her head. "Our legal people don't think there is much chance. Just from the advance marketing information I've gotten you can see that the design of the craft is quite different. However, the use and the target market are the same."

"You're the marketing expert, Carrie," I said. "Where does this leave us?"

"If CWS holds to their schedule, their boat will arrive at almost exactly the same time as ours. If that's the case, and they really are outspending us in advertising, we'll lose a significant edge in product differentiation and recognition. I can't tell you what that's going to mean in long term sales, but obviously we're looking at a different picture than before." She stopped and made a few notes. "Being first to the market is so important. Even if we could have a few months we would have a heavy duty advantage."

Ralph had been slowly coming to a boil as he listened to Carrie. "Damn!" he finally exploded. "We've already spent more than $250,000!" Thanks to my project costing, Ralph knew exactly how much money we had spent. He looked around the table for someone to blame. His eyes stopped on Stu. "You said that the WindSailor was the only product of its kind, Stuart."

Stu was not ready to be the scapegoat. "As you know, we surveyed the other European and even Asian manufacturers extensively. Like I said in my original report, there was some risk in proceeding with this, not the least of which was that someone could copy us more quickly than we thought."

Ralph did not want to let Stu off the hook. "But you practically guaranteed us 18 months without competition! Now we don't even have 18 days!" Ralph could be a great guy when things were going well, but he tended to turn nasty when things were not.

Carrie decided to step in and change the direction of the conversation. "We shouldn't be throwing in the towel yet. The market for this product is large, and our projections allow for us to make money even with competition. Granted, we didn't think it would be for two to three years."

Ralph turned to vent himself on Carrie. "Those first two years were going to be the payback for our up-front investment!"

Like Stu, Carrie was not about let Ralph shoot her down without a fight. "What about all those strategic reasons, like being on the cutting edge of the new product market, maintaining our name as a leading manufacturer, positioning ourselves for the future? Do you want to throw that out of the window?"

From the expression on Ralph's face, I would have guessed he would if it improved his next quarter's results. "Look," he said, "all that future crap is nice, but if we don't get our payback in the first two years, our performance looks like dirt." And there goes your promotion, I thought.

I decided to throw my hat into the ring. "Carrie, you keep coming back to the idea of being first into the market. What if we could be ready for the beginning of the buying season instead of June. How much of an advantage would that give us?"

Carrie's face brightened. "It might be 70 percent as good."

Ralph immediately seized on this possibility of salvation. "70 percent? If we have the WindSailor to the dealers by April?"

Carrie nodded. "It would mean changing our marketing campaign. We've got everything set to go for June, not April. We would have to refocus our efforts, but if I had a half-season head start, I could establish a significant advantage for Hyler."

Ralph turned to me. "Can we have the WindSailor by April?" Everyone else looked at me too.

I wasn't feeling as uneasy with that question as I would have without Martha's help. We had a coherent plan, one that was specified in such a way as to make it easy to do sensitivity analysis. Since we knew how all of the tasks went together, we could quickly see the results of shaving some time here and there. "I can find out fairly quickly."

Ralph stood up. "Then do it. We'll meet again tomorrow at 10 a.m. Carrie, make sure the marketing campaign can be shortened as well. Try to keep the cost down. We're already at the limit of our budget. Spending more money for less competitive advantage will not go over well with the board."

Scope, Schedule, Cost, and Quality

A smoke ring drifted by my ear. "If you're willing to spend a little more money, you can always make the execution a little shorter," Martha said.

Various members of the project team had spent the rest of the afternoon trying to tighten up our plan. We had found a few places to save time, but not enough to bring our finish date from June 23 to April 15.

"But, Martha, we've been over the plan several times and we ended up saving about a week and a half. We need to cut almost two more months!"

That didn't seem to bother her. "Like I said, Will, it can be done. It's just a question of money."

I said dejectedly, "Ralph doesn't want us to spend any extra money."

Martha picked up my pad of paper and a pencil and drew something.

"This is a picture that both you and your sponsor need to learn about, Willie," she said. "I've simplified things a little, but these four components roughly represent all the aspects of an assignment." She tapped each in turn as she elaborated. "Scope has to do with how much is in the assignment.

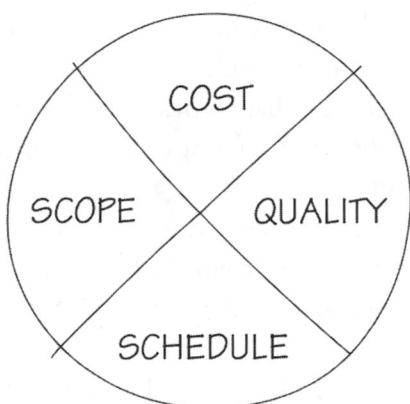

"Schedule has to do with how long things are going to take.

"Cost has to do with the price of disposable diapers versus cloth ones." I looked up at her quizzically. "Just seeing if you're awake, Willie." What a weird lady. "Actually, cost has to do with how much the whole assignment is going to cost.

"Finally, there's quality, the standard to which the assignment is performed.

"Every assignment is a system that operates within the constraints of all four components. And each one affects one or more of the others in a predictable way. For example, if the scope of work increases, what effect will it have on these other variables?"

I looked at the page. "Well, an increase in scope might increase the cost, or the assignment might take longer."

"Or both," Martha added. "Now what about cost? What if the budget for your assignment was suddenly cut?"

I had had lots of experience with that one. "Easy. You might have to decrease your scope and compromise your quality, or even take a little longer." Before she could say it, I added, "Or a mixture of all three."

"You're getting the picture, Will. Now let me ask you another question. Can you picture a situation in which one of these variables changes without affecting one or more of the other three?"

The way she said it, I thought it might be a trick question so I tried to visualize a situation where cutting the cost didn't affect something else. I found that I could.

"Actually, an assignment that I worked on back East had the budget cut. We still did the same amount of work, with the same quality, and not too far off schedule."

"Was your time charged against the assignment?"

"Well, no. None of the inside employees' time was. Why?"

"Did you find yourself working more hours than you planned to?"

Had she been there? "Yeah, I did. A lot more. We had planned to contract out a bunch of stuff, and when the budget got cut..." Suddenly I could see what she was getting at. "What you're saying is, we spent at least the same amount of money. It's just that our time didn't get charged to the project like a contractor's would. We really only cut costs on paper, not in reality."

Martha nodded. "That's exactly it. Having employees work unpaid overtime is a cost, whether you choose to account for it correctly or not. Now I ask you again, can you think of a situation where one of these variables changes without affecting the other three?"

The picture was clear now. "No," I said.

"Will, understanding the interaction of the components is to assignments what understanding the law of gravity is to designing buildings. You simply can't cheat. However, once you recognize the relationships, you can deal with things more effectively."

"So, Ralph's dream of not spending more money is just that, a dream."

"Not necessarily. However, if Ralph wants to shorten the schedule, there will have to be changes in one or more of the other three components."

I realized what she was getting at. "We could also cut the scope a little, or do a lower quality job, and not just spend more money."

"Right, Will. All the possibilities must be examined."

Crashing

"Now," she took her pipe out of her mouth, "we need to talk about crashing."

"Is this another test to see if I'm paying attention?"

Martha chuckled as she stuffed more tobacco into her pipe. "Crashing just happens to be the name for what you have to do now: make the project shorter." She studied her tobacco stuffing job. "The rules are simple but important. I'll start with a question. To decrease the duration of the project, what activities should you focus on making shorter?"

I thought for a minute. "I guess the ones you can shorten for the least money."

"Only partly right, Will. The activities you want to focus on all have a certain characteristic."

I had no idea until I visualized our dependency chart. "They are the critical activities, the ones that determine the length of the project. Otherwise you might spend money or cut tasks that don't affect the finish date at all."

I got a smoke ring in the face as a reward. "Correct, you must focus on the critical path. Now, how can you make those activities shorter?"

I thought about a simple activity like spreading topsoil where you want your front lawn to be. If I wanted to do it faster, I would add more people. Or I could change the scope by making the lawn smaller. Or I could change the quality by spreading the top soil thinner. Or I could hire a bulldozer to do it, instead of doing it by hand. "To shorten activities you could add resources, or reduce the scope of the task, or not do it as well, or even change the resource to a more productive one."

"Close enough," said Martha, "although remember that changes you make in each task affect all of the others. If you choose to do less during a particular task, you better make sure that it doesn't cause you problems down the line. Now what do you need to add more resources?"

That was easy. "Money. Something which I don't have a lot of."

That didn't bother Martha. "Yes, well, you still need to understand how to do it. Remember, you only have to tell your sponsor how to make the schedule shorter. It's his decision about the extra money, or decreased scope, or whatever."

Martha puffed on her pipe and looked out over the lawn for a few minutes and didn't say anything. Finally she turned back to me. "I think you understand what you need to do now, and I don't want to keep adding details that may confuse you, or that you may not need. However, there are two things to keep in mind about crashing projects. The first is that there is something called the *ultimate crash point*. It is the shortest time in which a task can be done. Adding resources at that point only costs more money and doesn't save you any time."

I tried to apply the idea of the ultimate crash point to my topsoil example. I visualized adding more and more people to the picture. As I reached 15, there started to be line-ups to get at the dirt pile. People started to get in each other's way. At 20, they needed a supervisor just to direct traffic. At 25, they formed a union and went on strike. I got the picture.

"The second thing is, as you shorten tasks, the critical path may change. Check the critical path each time you crash a task. Spending money to shorten non-critical tasks is stupid." That seemed pretty obvious, but I made a mental note to watch out for it. Martha had yet to steer me wrong.

I looked at my watch. It was nearing 10 p.m. I thought the chances of getting my project team together that night were slim. I'd call them at home and settle for an early morning meeting. I got up to go.

Martha said, "One more thing, Will," and hesitated.

"Yes?"

"You're doing...I think...It's nice that you listen to me." Before I could say anything, she tottered inside. I wasn't sure, but I thought she might have been paying me a compliment.

20

On a Crash Course

Crashing turned out to be tedious, even though the name made it sound exciting. We rolled Amanda's computer into the conference room, taped a printout of the dependency chart to the wall, and went to work. Everyone on the assignment team was there, as well as some of our "technical" experts" like Mark and Luigi.

The need to focus on the critical path made the choice of where to start simple. The tedious part was inputting changes, recalculating the schedules, finding the new critical path, and starting all over again on a new activity. We also had to save every combination of possible shortened schedules, and keep track of them for evaluation purposes. Once we added in potential scope changes, we created a myriad of combinations.

By 9:30 a.m. we had stopped creating new scenarios and started evaluating the ones we had, because at 10 I was supposed to have an answer for Ralph. When he and the others showed up at the door, I was sure I had an option that he couldn't turn down.

The New Schedule, the New Budget

The silence in the conference room told me we had pulled off a coup. I do not think anyone, especially Ralph, had expected the scenario I had just presented.

"Could you explain that one more time?" he asked in a puzzled voice. "I still don't believe we can have the first run of WindSailors ready by April 15, and it's going to cost us less money."

I was quick to qualify his statement. "That's right, Ralph, but as you can see," here I gestured to the dependency chart on the wall, "we have decreased the scope of the project a little. We won't be paving the new employee parking lot this season. The same is true for the new public parking lot and access road, which will have to be approved by the city council. We also won't have the entire assignment finished by the fifteenth of April. The new fencing between us and Lake Hyler won't be done until our original date in June, and the same goes for the new retail outlet." I looked back at Ralph. "We shortened up the delivery of part of the project—the production facilities—but not all of the other components will be ready by then."

This didn't seem to concern Ralph, which is what I expected, and Carrie was pleased as well. Stu said, "You didn't really answer Ralph's question, Will. Why is this new plan costing less?"

"Two reasons," I told him as if I had understood this all my life. "The first, and largest, has to do with the decreased scope. We have to speed up the construction, machine installation, and worker training activities to get the production facilities done on time. That actually increases our costs. As you can see on the plan, installation and training will require three shifts instead of one, and we're doing construction on two shifts. That means more money in shift differentials, instructors, insurance premiums, equipment, all kinds of things. The net result is that, while we cut a lot of time off the finish date, we need more money to do it. To make up for that extra money, we went looking for scope changes that wouldn't affect the end product. We stumbled on paving, which is horrendously expensive. Dropping the paving saved more money than crashing the other activities cost.

Of course, paving, whenever it gets done, will have to be part of some other budget." I didn't say it, but having a plan made it easy (even possible) for us to discover this.

"Will, you said there were two reasons why the cost went down." Leave it to Stu not to miss a trick.

"In fact, the second reason is fairly minor. As construction activities got shorter, the overhead costs associated with them actually went down instead of up."

"What costs would those be?" Ralph asked.

"Things like supervision and clerical support. They didn't have to be provided for as long, and therefore that portion of the cost went down." I had almost not noticed this cost decrease, but I thought it was important to mention.

"Wait a minute," Ralph said. "You're telling me that contracting companies actually lowered their bid prices when you told them to do the job more quickly?" Ralph was a suspicious kind of guy.

"No," I conceded. "The contractors haven't agreed at this point, although we are going to try to get them to reduce that portion of their cost. The savings come from the reduction in our staff hours supervising the contractor." Ralph seemed impressed that I had gone to that level of detail. The savings had been minor, but money is money, and because of the way we had specified the contracts (we required dependency charts and costs by activity), I was confident that our contractors would not get the better of us.

Ralph looked at me, then at Carrie and Stu. Finally he looked back at me again. "I can't see a problem here. Can anyone point one out for me?"

Carrie asked me, "You're sure that you will be ready for April 15?" I nodded. "How many days to produce the first 400 boards?"

I shook my head. "I hate to abdicate responsibility, but that is not part of my assignment. Luigi Delgarno is the person to talk to for that." Carrie looked a little annoyed, so I told her "He tells me that he'll be ready with that number by May 1. But you better confirm that with him, it ain't my job."

"I don't see how I can turn this down, Will," Ralph told me. "My only question might be why the original plan didn't look like this?"

"The constraints have changed, Ralph, and that changes the plan. Here, let me show you something." I drew Martha's circle with scope, cost, quality, and schedule in the quadrants. After my explanation of how all the things interrelated Ralph grunted.

"Seems pretty obvious. But all that theoretical stuff aside, I like the new plan. I want you to proceed." He got up to leave.

"Uh, one more thing, Ralph," I told him. "This changes the objective statement, and I need your signed approval." I handed him an objective statement that we had revised just before the meeting.

"I suppose you want to make sure it's my head on the block, not yours." That was not exactly the point, but I didn't bother to correct him. He pointed his pen at me when he finished writing. "Just make sure that you are ready for production by April 15."

Things were frantic over the next couple of days. Amanda worked hard to secure the city council's approval of the delay in paving the parking lot and access roads. In the end we had to commit to paving by the beginning of next season. I admit I was thinking it won't be my problem by then, which was selfish of me.

Sheila and I got the contractors to agree about completing the work in less time without charging us an arm and a leg more. Fortunately we had their dependency charts to work from, which meant they could charge us extra only where they showed us it would cost extra.

The biggest crisis occurred in Marketing. All of the promotional literature for the roll-out to the dealers had already been printed, and four-color brochures are expensive. Ralph blew his stack over that one, but in the end the money my team saved was transferred to the Marketing budget and everyone came out of it okay. I guess Carrie wasn't paying attention to the scope, quality, cost, schedule circle when I explained it to Ralph.

By February 10 we were officially on a "crash course" toward April 15. All of the contracts had been renegotiated, the city had agreed to the lack of pavement, and even Marketing had promised to come through with the product name, logos, and decorative styling to meet our accelerated schedule. All that was left was to actually do it. As I discovered that time, and many since, that turned out to be a lot simpler than I expected. Of course, the execution wasn't without its share of difficulties.

A Contractor with An Opinion

"If you don't get your candy-ass people off my site and let me get this goddamn job done, I'll pull my men out of here and let you build it yourself!"

"Afternoon, Bud," I said. I couldn't think of anything else to say. Bud Zalansky was the prime contractor for our construction work, and prime contractor for just about all of the work that went on around Enderby. If there was a building going up in this area, you could bet that old Bud had a hand in it. He had been a fixture on the commercial and residential construction scene for almost thirty years, and right now I had a feeling the fixture was going to let go from the ceiling and crash down on my head.

"Don't 'afternoon' me," he growled. "You've got people all over me trying to tell me how to do things." He spat on the ground as he tried to wrestle his pants up over his impossibly huge gut.

Until today I had not dealt directly with any of the construction contractors. That was no accident; they intimidated the hell out of me. So I left that to Sheila.

I looked up into Bud's grizzled face. "I'm not sure I understand the problem, Bud." I looked back down at his chest. The view was less disturbing.

"Aren't you listening, son? You got a bunch of know-it-alls running around here telling me my business and I don't like it." He produced a pack of cigarettes from somewhere in his jeans and shook one out. "Let me tell you, Hyler was a better place when Al Burton was here. Now there was a man you could deal with."

The mention of Al's name irked me. "Look, Bud, my people jump all over you when you don't stick to the plan."

"That's the problem, Will," Sheila said, "he's not paying any attention to the dependency chart."

By the way he looked at her, I could tell that Bud wasn't a feminist. "That plan is just for general reference," he told me. "Things change when you're working on the site. Experience is my guide." He lit his cigarette and tossed the match on the ground.

"I'm sorry you feel that way Bud," I told him, "but we don't agree. And if you check your contract you'll see that you'll stick to the plan or you won't get paid. If you do deviate from the plan, you have to tell us why, and what the impact will be."

Bud just stared at me as he took a drag on his cigarette. Finally he said, "If I had known that I woulda looked a little closer at the damn thing."

"A little closer?" I echoed.

"About the planning part." Bud could smoke a cigarette without actually touching it with his fingers. As he talked it just kind of bobbed along on his lip. I couldn't take my eyes off it.

"Who did the plan for you, then?" I asked.

Bud gestured toward Sheila. "She did."

"Well?" I prompted.

"Well what?" she asked. "After we crashed the project Bud didn't want to be bothered with redoing his plan, so I did it for him."

I turned back to Bud. "And you didn't look too closely at the plan she produced?"

Bud laughed. "Never heard anyone so picky as you about stickin' to some stupid plan. Anyway, what's your problem? We'll get your stuff finished on time."

I turned back to Sheila. "Forgetting for a moment how the plan was arrived at, just what is Bud doing incorrectly?"

"I ain't doing nothing incorrectly," Bud interrupted.

I corrected myself. "What is Bud doing that is not according to plan, that will cause the construction to finish late and," I turned to look into Bud's grizzled face again, "which will cause Bud not to be paid?"

Sheila pointed toward the trailer that was serving as the construction supervision shack. "I can show you better if we look at the plan." The three of us walked over to the trailer in silence.

Inside, Sheila pointed to the dependency chart on the wall. "Bud's got a third of his crew out there working on getting the base for the fencing prepared, and he's planning to pour the concrete and set the poles in two days."

The dependency chart logic showed a number of things to be completed before that took place, including removing most of the heavy equipment from the expansion site. A glance out the window confirmed that that had yet to be done.

I looked at Bud. "Well?"

Bud sniffed. "You wanted this project speeded up. I'm doing the fencing now so we don't have to do it at the end."

I looked back at the dependency chart. "Fencing isn't on the critical path Bud. Why are you wasting people on that?"

Bud stared nearsightedly at the chart. "Well, uh." I wasn't sure he even knew what a critical path looked like, but he seemed worried.

"And," said Sheila, "when you go to take your heavy equipment out, you're going to have to make a hole in the fence."

"No, we won't. We'll just walk it out the main entrance of the plant."

"Only if you pay for the damage," Sheila shot back. "That road is paved. If you walk your equipment over it, it'll wreck the pavement."

Bud wasn't out of answers yet. "Then we'll bring in a flat bed and truck it out."

Sheila wasn't finished either. "Did you notice you didn't bring your equipment in that way, Bud? The road through the plant is short and twisted and there are a bunch of overhead wires. You can't get your truck through there and you can't get it back out with equipment on it."

Bud went back to peering nearsightedly at the plan and not saying anything.

I decided to sum up the situation. "Let me see if I've got this right, Bud. By ignoring the plan, you were about to spend a bunch of money crashing an activity that wasn't going to speed up the finish of the project. You were then going to spend even more money getting your equipment out, either by knocking down part of your newly constructed fence or repaving our road. Meanwhile resources are diverted from critical activities. All of which would have cost us our completion date, and therefore you a lot of money." Bud continued staring at the plan.

I softened my tone. "Look, Bud, I'm not trying to play a game of right and wrong. We have every confidence in your abilities as a contractor, but we're dealing with a very tight deadline and a complex situation. It's just too complicated to keep inside someone's head. Even one as experienced as yours." Bud finally looked at me. "Can you work with the plan?" I asked. "And," I added as an afterthought, "with Sheila?"

Bud nodded. "Thanks," I told him, "I'll leave you and Sheila to go over the details."

Sheila told me later that Bud couldn't get over the fact that we actually wanted him to work from a plan. According to him, that just wasn't part of the construction business. She figured that she hadn't converted him to dependency charts yet, but that he would at least stick to the one on this job. "I think when you said it would cost him money not to follow the plan you really got his attention."

Who Gets Rewarded?

By the evening of March 25, I was sitting on my in-laws' porch, enjoying the spring that was already well under way, and remarking on the surprising smoothness of the execution. Martha just chuckled. "Just like everyone else, Will, you probably expected that the execution would be the most stressful time of all."

"That's how it has always been for me in the past! Now I'm nervous because everything is going so well."

"That's an attitude you're going to have to change, Willie," she told me as she crammed some tobacco into her pipe. "With proper preparation, the execution should be boring, with no surprises. It's better that way, because the execution is where most of the money gets spent." She paused. "Why is it so difficult for people to understand? A clearly defined assignment followed by a well specified design and a detailed, useful execution plan results in a boring, as-planned, execution."

"Well, I suppose—"

"I'll tell you why, Will," she continued as if I wasn't there. "Society rewards those who are incompetent enough to create crises, and then lucky enough to muddle through them. We don't reward planned success; we want the quick fix, the lucky break, the Slim-Quick-Easy-Diet Solution!" Martha was almost starting to foam at the mouth, so I thought I should try and calm her down.

"That may be true, Martha, but I'm getting nothing but praise from the higher-ups at Hyler. They're very impressed with what your ideas have allowed us to accomplish."

"Humph!" Martha grunted, but I could see that she was pleased with the compliment.

"The interesting thing is, we've had lots of little crises during the execution, but having the detailed plan has allowed us to deal with them quickly and effectively. Our production facilities should be in operation by April 15, and I'll be finished everything by about June 1. I'm looking forward to getting back to my regular job."

Martha said, "Will, you've done a good job so far, but it isn't over yet. If I were you, I wouldn't be thinking ahead to June 1 as the end of your involvement with the WindSailor."

I swallowed. "Why do you say that, Martha?"

Martha smiled at my discomfort. "No particular reason, Willie. It's just that in my experience, people who have success at certain things are thought to have special abilities." She paused and puffed on her pipe. "Just remember, you do have some special abilities now, and in a similar situation, you can apply them with the same success."

I didn't like the sound of that, but Martha wouldn't tell me any more. By 10 the next morning I was starting to think that Martha might be psychic.

21

A
New Assignment

"Frankly, I'm a little surprised, "Ralph said. "When we lost Al Burton, I thought this project might flounder." I glanced quickly at Stu, but resisted the urge to smirk openly. "Anyway, Marketing now tells us that they believe Ms. Starblanket's prediction regarding our early entry into the market to be correct. So despite getting caught totally off-guard by California Water Trends, things are definitely looking up."

"Now, I didn't call you in here just to compliment you on your success so far. I have what you would call a scope change. Or maybe even a whole new assignment." My heart sank. More work, just like Martha said.

Ralph said, "Don't look so glum, Will. This isn't punishment, it's a reward."

Resigned, I asked, "Just what is the 'this' you're talking about, Ralph?"

"Marketing wants to rollout the WindSailor to the dealers in a grand way, something they've never tried before. Instead of the usual 'take it to the dealers' approach, they want to organize a kind of boat show and regatta on Hyler Lake for the weekend of June 6 and 7, and bring all of the major dealers on the West Coast in for a look. The dealers can see how the product is manufactured, and have a sail with it themselves."

"This all sounds great, but what do you need me for?" I asked.

Ralph smiled and said, "I want you to organize it."

"Why me? It's Marketing's show!"

"The people in Marketing have a lot on their plate. You'll have the time available, and you've demonstrated that you have the skills as well." Ralph stood up to leave. "Stuart will be the sponsor of this project. Don't worry," he held up his hand to cut off my question. "He has all the necessary spending authority. Believe it or not, I've learned a few things about being a sponsor over the last eight months. As I'm sure you recognize, time is short on this one, so I recommend you get started as soon as possible." With that, he left the room.

I glared at Stu. "This is all your fault."

Stu held up his hands. "Not me, buddy," he said. "This is 100 percent your fault. Believe me, if your assignment hadn't been going as well as it has, you wouldn't be in this position. That, and the fact that Marketing has been screwing up big-time on their part of the Wind-Sailor. Notice how I'm the sponsor, not Carrie? Believe me, Will, I'm about as happy with this as you are."

"Your unhappiness doesn't really help me much, Stu. I mean, I don't know anything about arranging boat shows."

As usual, Stu wasn't interested in excuses. "You didn't know anything about production facilities or construction work. And I'll bet you still don't, do you?"

I had to admit it was true. "But I had technical people who knew about those things."

"And you'll have technical people on this one too. Ralph's line about the people in Marketing being busy is mostly bull. What else do they have to do now except get ready for this show? All you have to do is organize this thing like you did the last one, and everyone will be happy."

I sighed. "I suppose I don't have a lot of choice, do I?"

"You could quit." He gave me a silly grin and passed me a piece of paper. On it was a list of names. "I took the liberty of suggesting who you might want on your project team. I've slotted them into the roles that your consultant suggested. You can make whatever changes you want. Like Ralph, I recommend you get started right away."

Doing this One Right

We had the first project team meeting that day, and following Martha's process, produced our first objective statement. I met with Stu the next morning and he signed it.

As it turned out, most of the design process had already been completed by the marketing folks. Mind you, it wasn't in a very presentable format, but now that I understood a little about how the design process worked and what it was supposed to produce, we had no difficulty generating a good, detailed design inside of three days. It described exactly what the situation would be like the moment before we opened the show.

Stu signed that off quickly as well.

Next we created the execution plan, which turned out to be every bit as complicated as the one for remodeling the plant. I was amazed at the number of activities that go into organizing something of this nature. Through it all, I simply acted as facilitator to ensure the process flowed smoothly. Once my new project team got used to the idea that I wanted—make that *needed*—their input, things went well.

For our first pass at the dependency chart, I borrowed Amanda to help input the plan to the project management software. Time was of the essence, and she had developed a very slick two-person procedure for transferring the information from the planning board. We hadn't forgotten our horrendous first experience with inputting the plan to the computer.

After all of the activities and resources had been input, we discovered that we could be ready to go by June 5, as required, but that it was going to cost more than Stu had in his budget. Happily, I knew that this was Stu's problem, and his decision to make, not mine. Seven days after the assignment had been passed to me, Stu signed off the execution plan, approving the increased budget. We were off and running.

Like all momentous occasions, the fifteenth was a day of both joy and sorrow. There was joy because we handed the newly completed production facilities over to Luigi and his crew. The sorrow? There was no champagne. The crews simply went on regular shift at 8:00 a.m. in the morning and began producing WindSailors. I watched for awhile, until Luigi shooed me away, telling me he had everything under control.

More sorrow came in the form of complications with the rapidly approaching Boat Show and Regatta. The news sailed into my office with Leslie Frame.

"Will! Great news! We've got Buster McKay!" she told me breathlessly. She looked as if she had run all the way from her office.

"Wonderful!" I said. "Who's Buster McKay?"

"He's our celebrity endorsement! You remember."

I did remember. The whole idea of celebrity guest selection had made me nervous when it went into the project plan. The marketing folks had told me it was important to have a role model or "opinion leader" to recommend our product. When I pointed out that the WindSailor was supposed to appeal to the novice, or to people who weren't very good, and that there probably weren't too many famous sailors or windsurfers who fell into those categories, they weren't interested. According to them, it didn't matter if the opinion leader actually used our product, the person simply had to be well known and 'in vogue'.

The fact that we didn't have a celebrity, and the fact that my project team wanted to build the finding of one into the execution plan, did not please me. My brief experience with systematic planning of projects had indicated that there shouldn't be a lot of uncertainties by the time the execution plan is created. To me, selecting a celebrity endorser was uncertain at best, and part of the design.

However, Leslie was telling me that I had worried for nothing. "So is this Buster going to meet our needs?" I asked.

"Absolutely! In fact, he is better than we hoped. He's a local boy from Crescent City, California."

"That's local?"

"It's West Coast, and that's close enough. Anyway, he's won the Windsurfing World Cup for three of the last five years. He even does color commentary on TV for some events. And he's had bit parts in a few beach movies, so his recognition factor is high. The best part is, he's got a six year old son."

"So?" I am obviously not a marketing person at heart.

"Don't you see?" Leslie exclaimed. "His boy is still too small for a regular windsurfer. We'll get Buster teaching his son how to sail the WindSailor! It gives his endorsement a real ring of truth."

"I thought whether or not the celebrity used the product wasn't important."

Leslie gave me an exasperated look. "You really can be a wet blanket, you know that, Will? No, it isn't an absolute requirement, but it doesn't hurt. Anyway, you should be happy. We've got our celebrity ahead of schedule."

I wasn't ready to celebrate just yet. "Does Buster fit into our budget?"

Leslie got a guilty look on her face. "Not exactly, but we need to sign him right away. Coppertone wants him to do a promotion that same weekend."

After a hasty meeting with Stu, we increased our budget again.

And so it went. Little crises presented themselves, were resolved, and we continued.

The Launch

"Would the owner of the lime green BMW, license plate SAIL4U, please return to your vehicle. Your car is blocking access to the hot-dog stand!" The PA system was blaring right in my ear so I led the kids away to a quieter spot.

It was the second day of our WindSailor extravaganza and I was getting tired of public outings in general and this one in particular. The only thing that kept me going was the knowledge that today marked the end of my project responsibilities. My work on the first assignment had ended the previous Thursday when we finished up our new retail facility next to Hyler Lake, and pulled out the temporary access to the employee parking lot. Technically, my responsibilities for the product launch were finished too, but I had to be around until the end to make sure that everything went off okay.

Suddenly a large bald man wearing too much cologne was pumping my arm. "Will Campbell!" he said effusively. "Damned glad to meet you! My name is Biff Flagstaff. I own the Sports Trends chain of stores. I think this WindSailor thing is the best damn idea you folks have ever had, and this is the best damn way to tell people about it I've ever seen. I just had to congratulate the man in charge. Stu Barnes over there said you were the man responsible."

I looked over to where Stu was standing with his wife, and he gave me an elfish grin. "Thank you, Mr. Flagstaff," I said modestly. "I'm glad you're enjoying yourself." I thought I'd put in a mild sales pitch. "I hope the WindSailor will be one of your top sellers this summer."

"I'm sure it will, Will. I'm sure it will, Will." While I tried to unscramble the alliterative repetition, Biff switched his attention to Jenny and the kids. "And this is your fine family I assume?" It was a rhetorical question because he introduced himself. "I'm Biff Flagstaff, Mrs. Campbell. Very pleased to meet you."

"Likewise," said Jenny with more than a hint of sarcasm in her voice. I gave her a be-nice-to-the-customers look, but Biff didn't notice. He was kneeling down in front of Jake and Sarah.

"Watch my hand closely," he told them. He waved his hand around and then reached behind Jake's ear and pulled out a piece of bubble gum. Biff handed it to Jake and with his other hand he pulled a chocolate coin out of Sarah's nose. Both kids smiled shyly.

"What do you say?" Jenny prompted.

"Thank you, mister," the kids replied almost in unison.

Biff stood up and turned to me. "Fine family you have here, Will. And a fine new product." He shook my hand again and strode off towards another knot of people.

Jenny stared after him. "Biff? What kind of a name is that? I'm glad you're not doing this marketing stuff full-time. It can be very tiresome. That guy is an idiot." My wife does beat around the bush.

"He owns 43 sporting goods retail outlets that specialize in sailing and boating products."

"So, he's a rich idiot," Jenny said.

"I like him, Dad," Sarah told me. "He's nice."

By half-past seven that evening, things had pretty much wound down. The hot dogs and hamburgers had been eaten, and most people were regretting the last three. The barbecue pits were nothing but smoking embers, and the beer had been drunk, and most people would be regretting the last three of those later.

Ralph, Stu, Carrie, Leslie, and I stood together at the edge of the lake as Carrie gave us her assessment of the event.

"The dealers loved it! No one has done anything like this before."

"Sure, everyone had a good time," Ralph said. "But how do you think that will translate into actual sales?"

"I don't think, Ralph, I know." Carrie paused for dramatic effect. "As of right now we have verbal commitments for 2,700 WindSailors for this summer."

"That's more than 100 percent of our capacity!" Stu pointed out.

"Not my problem. I just sell 'em. I let you folks worry about delivering them."

"Now that is good news, Carrie," Ralph said. "You're right, we'll worry about the extra capacity. You just keep selling them."

Carrie turned to me. "We really should be thanking you, Will. To be honest, I had my reservations about having a non-marketing person organize this event. But you surprised me! Except for Buster McKay twisting his ankle on that beer can, it could not have run more smoothly."

"Well," I said, trying to sound modest, " I just helped put the idea in place. It was your concept, really." I could see that Carrie appreciated me giving some of the praise back, especially in front of Ralph. It was easy to do because it was the truth. It was her idea, and all I did was to organize it systematically. I was beginning to learn that those two facets of an assignment were very different.

"Will," Ralph said, putting his hand on my shoulder, "Good job! You've really come through for Hyler. In fact we've been talking about trying to make better use of your project management skills. That's something we'll discuss next week. For now, though, I guess you're officially finished both assignments."

But as Martha pointed out the next day, that wasn't quite true.

Part Six

The Review Process

22

Assessing Assignments

"Not done? We got the production facilities on-line, everything is operating normally, I even finished the extra assignment. What do you mean, I'm not done?"

Martha just sat there, smoking her pipe. Finally she said, "Apparently you've forgotten all about the framework of an assignment. So, let me ask you a question: How do you improve your ability to do something?"

I thought for a minute. "Practice. You do the thing over and over, until you get good."

"That's right," said Martha. "You do something again and again, each time changing how you do it, because, as we agreed some time ago, you can't do something better unless you do it differently." She paused to send a smoke ring out over the porch railing. "What do you need to have frequently to help you improve?"

"Success?" I ventured.

"Not necessarily. What you need is the thing that tells you whether you're having success."

"I have no idea what you're talking about."

Martha grunted. "I guess your short term success has gone to your head, Willie, leaving no room for common sense. Not that there was a lot of room to begin with." She scowled before she finally told me. "Feedback! Feedback is what you need to improve. How can you tell if what you're doing is the right thing if you don't get any feedback? How can you improve how you do something without feedback? You can't!"

I gave her what I hoped to be a condescending stare. "Don't you think that's a little self-evident, Martha? I was looking for something that I didn't already know."

Martha was not impressed. "If you know all about feedback, Willie, perhaps you can explain to me why you think you are finished your assignment."

I started to say, "Because all of the work is done," but then I finally understood what she was saying. "You're telling me that we need more feedback on the assignment?" Martha nodded. "And that getting that feedback is the final stage in the assignment?" Martha nodded again. "But what else is there to know? We finished on time, only slightly over budget, and the production facilities work."

"Your problem, Willie, like everyone else's, is that you don't look beyond the short term, the immediate. Look, let's review our picture again." She picked up the pad of paper wrote some familiar words:

GENESIS

DESIGN

EXECUTION PLAN

EXECUTION

REVIEWS:
    1. Acceptance of the Deliverables
    2. Assessment of Project Management
    3. Evaluation of the Original Concept

"We haven't talked about the review process yet, but it is just as important as all of the others, although it is usually done in as perfunctory a manner as you have done it, so a lot of the benefit is lost." She turned to me. "Now, Willie, just like we've done for the other phases, I want you to answer a simple question: What should be the result of the review phase?"

After all of the talk about feedback, I could hardly get this one wrong. "Information or feedback about how to improve the way assignments get done."

Martha blew a congratulatory smoke ring in my direction. "And few people want to spend time looking back at an assignment. For better or worse, it's done. What do you suppose happens when that attitude prevails?"

I had only to look at my own past. "The same mistakes, except maybe the biggest ones, get repeated."

Martha nodded. "They do, indeed. And as you know, a combination of many little mistakes make big things go wrong. Without a review, the little things get forgotten or missed. What about the good things?"

"What good things?"

Martha looked at me over the top of her bifocals. "Don't be so cynical, Willie. Good things happen on every assignment too."

"Like the bad things, only major successes are remembered. The little stuff gets forgotten." I had always found that good things were forgotten, but mistakes haunted you forever.

"Yes, things do get done right, but if no one gets recognition for them, they may not do the right things next time. So you agree that a review is important?"

I had a Marthaesque answer for that. "Only if you want to improve how you do assignments."

"There is hope for you yet, Will. Now, do you want to improve the way you and Hyler manage assignments?"

"Of course." I don't know why I agreed, it certainly was not in my job description.

Martha nodded with satisfaction. "Well, then, let's talk about the review process in more detail." She turned the pad around so that she could draw on it, and added some lines to what she already had.

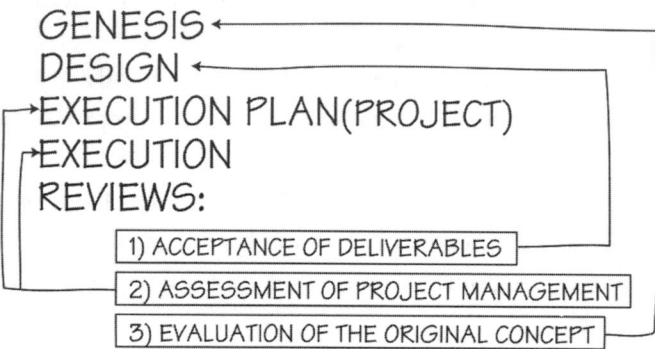

"There are three stages to the review process, and each stage is simply a series of questions to be answered. The answers provide the feedback, and the basis for improving the next assignment." She traced the line she had drawn from the first review up to the design stage. "This first review is all about accepting the deliverable. This is the simplest one because there is only one question to be asked: To what extent does the deliverable match the design?"

I stared at it for a second and then said, "Shouldn't the question be more along the lines of: Is the deliverable acceptable?"

"No, Willie, that comes later. You see, the design was approved by the sponsor, and if done properly, the users. All we want to know is, did we deliver what we said we would?"

I thought about this. "If the production facilities were all working, the staff was hired and trained, and all the new computer systems were up and running, I'd say we passed this one with flying colors."

"It's usually not a completely black and white answer. Was everything perfect when you handed over the production facilities?"

There were still a few bugs in the inventory software and some of our new hires had already washed out. And some of the interior finishing on the factory additions was incomplete. "There was a bunch of little stuff that wasn't quite finished, but we got all of the important things done," I said, a little defensively.

Martha smiled her knowing smile. "That's how it is at the finish of all executions. Small things here and there need to be tidied up or redone. The extent to which those things are minor or unimportant is what this review is all about. In your assignment it sounds like those little things aren't a problem. The second review—I think of it as the review of project management—looks at the planning and execution. The questions that need to be asked are straightforward. For example," Martha paused.

We sat in silence for about 30 seconds and I started to think that maybe Martha had had a stroke. Finally I realized that she was waiting for me to provide some questions. "Oh, sorry. Let's see. How about questions about the plan? How accurate was it? Was the logic correct? Were the contingency plans good?" Martha motioned for me to go on.

"Well, was it completed on time? On budget? Were all items in the scope done?" Um, I decided to let loose and free associate. "Was the plan kept up to date? Was the sponsor kept informed? Was the plan revised when major changes occurred? Was the objective statement revised? Were the team members kept informed? How was morale? Who shot JFK? That kind of thing."

Martha nodded. "Very simple questions, aren't they? Taking the time to ask them and record the answers is a very simple way of improving assignments. Now the third review, the review of the original idea." She leaned forward and continued in a subdued voice. "The third review almost never gets done. Do you know why?" I shook my head. "Because," she said, her voice suddenly loud, "once you've spent $2 million building a new factory, you'd like to think it was a good idea!" Martha smiled and sat back in her chair.

"By the time you reach senior management level in corporate America, you've gotten damn good at covering your mistakes. This third review goes back to the sponsor level to ask if the whole thing was a good idea in the first place. A lot of sponsors don't like that. It should be, but seldom is, part of the strategic planning process."

I was impressed, but I could see a problem. "It'll be two or three seasons until we know if the WindSailor is a hit."

"That's exactly right, Will! The third review is at a much more strategic level and often takes some time to complete. However, if we want to continue to generate good ideas, or to avoid bad ones, we have to ask: Was the objective of the assignment appropriate?"

"Who is going to review the WindSailor idea? Ralph is the president of the company, as well as my sponsor. Don't you think he might be a little biased?"

"How about your board of directors?"

Actually, I thought, that's exactly who should do the review. Ralph's promotional hopes were riding with the Hyler board, and the success or failure of the WindSailor would probably be a big part of their decision.

As Martha ran a pipe cleaner through her pipe, she said, "It isn't supposed to be the Spanish Inquisition though. In my experience, using the review process to point fingers has a net negative result. Treat it as an opportunity for the project team and sponsor to learn. The review questions should lead to productive answers for future assignments, and they should be asked all the way through an assignment. It's no good waiting until the very end to tell someone about a little thing they did two months ago. However, the formal review process is important to close out an assignment, and highlight the lessons learned."

Another Assignment?

"I'll talk to Ralph," Stu promised me. "I think he'll be interested. He loves everything you do these days, Will."

I was sitting in Stu's office, telling him about my recommendations for a formal project review. Thanks to my talk with Martha, I had decided that maybe my job description did include a little project management improvement.

Stu continued. "The Hyler board met again last night in New York. Ralph flew in to give them an update on the WindSailor and I guess they were fairly happy with how things are going, even if we aren't going to meet our projected return on investment." The advent of competition was expected to reduce the assignment's projected ROI. It was still healthy enough. And that, combined with the benefit of continuing to position Hyler on the cutting edge of the small-craft sailing world, meant everyone was pleased about the decision to pursue it.

"Ralph did mention something that he wanted me to discuss with you, Will. We both agree that you managed this assignment, both assignments really, in a different way. I know that you've been telling your project team that you've been using an outside consultant, but I also know that you haven't spent any money on consulting fees."

"Well, um," I started to explain, but Stu held up his hand.

"I understand the trick. Sometimes if you want to introduce a new idea it's easier to say it was someone else's. I've done it myself. But I think you're on to something here, and we want to start managing all our assignments like you did. So what Ralph and I would like you to do is create a procedure manual that details the process you worked out for this project. Nothing too long and complicated, but something that captures the essence of what you did."

Perfect. The more success I had, the more work I got. Here I was, looking forward to anonymous retirement from project management, and now I was being asked to write a company procedure manual. "I don't know, Stu, I'm way behind in my other work. And besides, you know what I think of procedure manuals. People just look at them and fall asleep."

Stu looked amused. "I'm afraid you're stuck with it, Will. I'll tell you what. Don't make it a standard procedure manual. Use your imagination. But give us something. We don't want to lose this process."

The Team Wraps Up

I called my project team together later that day to wrap things up, and to let them know about the upcoming review. As had become our tradition, we met over donut holes and coffee at the Dunkin' Donuts.

"Review?" Sheila said. "Inquisition is more like it, don't you think?"

"Yeah," agreed Amanda. "I hate report cards. They're so impersonal."

Mark Goldman did his part to cheer everyone up. "Maybe California Water Sports is already taking market share."

"Actually, I've got some news about them," Leslie told us. We all turned toward her expectantly. "Apparently they were a little optimistic. It looks like their WindSailor knock-off won't be on the market this season."

I forgot all about the review. "You're kidding. You mean we went to all that trouble and now they're not even going to introduce their product this year?" I was not sure whether to be happy or upset.

Leslie smiled. "Relax! We didn't spend that much more money. And anyway, we just found that out today, so there was nothing we could have done."

"What happened?" Amanda asked.

"Something about design problems they didn't discover until after they had installed their new production equipment. We're starting to get orders from their unhappy customers!" Leslie took a donut hole and toasted us all.

"I wonder if Al Burton is looking for another job," Sheila wondered out loud. She was still "temporarily" assigned to his position.

I tried to get things back in focus. "Folks, back to the review process. We can't improve how we do things if we don't have an objective look at our performance, and the review process does just that." Everyone looked skeptical. "Hey, everything has gone well so far, hasn't it?" They all nodded grudgingly. "Trust me, this won't be any different. And I've got something to help us prepare." I handed everyone a sheet of paper.

"These are the questions I've submitted to Ralph to be used during the review session. Over the next few days I want each of you to think about them in terms of our just completed assignment. We'll meet before the session with Ralph to talk about our answers."

"Isn't that cheating?" Alice asked.

I smiled. "Not really. I want to make sure we all get something out of this process. We won't depend entirely on Ralph to give it to us."

All the donut holes were gone and the coffee was drunk. Nothing was left but the check. "Before you go, I just wanted to say something. This assignment has been different for me, and I guess for you too. We tried out some new ideas in a do-or-die situation, and they worked. And in the process, I think we all, and me especially, learned something about doing assignments. I'm grateful that we didn't have personal problems working together, and that you were all so competent and professional. We were able to focus on the bigger picture of doing this assignment without getting bogged down in the little stuff." I paused, and dabbed my eye with a napkin. "Thanks for everything, guys."

There was a moment of silence, and then Sheila spoke for everyone when she said, "Are you paying for this?"

Part Seven

The Project Manager's Survival Manual

23

Recording the Fundamentals

"Daddy, why don't you come outside and play with Jake and me?" Sarah asked me as I slumped in front of our home computer.

"Jake and I, honey," I corrected.

"What?" she looked at me questioningly.

"You should say 'Jake and I,' not 'Jake and me.'"

"She was right the first time," Jenny called from the kitchen.

I looked at Sarah and she laughed. "Why don't you go outside and play, and I'll come out and join you in a minute."

I got up and walked into the kitchen with what I hoped was a sufficiently ferocious look on my face. "Dear, how many times have I told you not to embarrass me in front of the children?"

Jenny laughed, just like Sarah. I said, "Let me tell you about one of my favorite quotes. It goes like this: 'Any man can support me when I'm right. What I want is a man who will support me when I'm wrong.' You can just substitute 'woman' for man."

"Who said it?"

"I think you're missing the point."

Jenny laughed again. "But Sarah was right. I didn't want her to learn the wrong way from her dad. In 12 years she might be valedictorian for her graduating class and she'd make a mistake in her speech thanks to you, and be embarrassed about it forever. It would ruin her self-esteem. And she'd probably resent you for the rest of your days. You should be thanking me from saving you from a fate worse than death."

As I tried in vain to come up with a sufficiently snappy comeback, Jenny turned back to the dishes. I gave up trying and grabbed a dish towel to help her dry.

"You don't have to do that, honey," she told me. "I know you have to get those project management procedures written. I'll finish up here."

"You don't understand, Jen. Drying dishes has suddenly become the most fascinating thing in the world, given the alternative." I held a glass up to the light to check for errant moisture.

"Getting writer's block?" Jenny asked.

"Not really, hon. I would have to have written something to be able to first call myself a writer. Then when I got blocked it would be writer's block. Since I haven't written a thing since I was asked to do this over two weeks ago, I would say I have mental paralysis."

"So what's the problem?"

"There just seems to be so much to tell. It would take me at least a couple hundred pages to explain it all. And if I did that, it would be boring as hell." I put my now well-dried second glass up on the shelf.

"The thing that really bothers me is the idea of detailed procedures. Every situation is different, and that means that just about every detailed procedure is going to be a little bit wrong in every new situation. And policies are worse. They are designed to make sure that people don't think for themselves."

Jenny frowned at me. "I don't understand."

"Let me give you an example. At the start of this assignment, Ralph wanted me to do earned value costing. That's a specific way of reporting costs on projects. But that method includes a whole lot of cost indexes and reporting formats that made absolutely no sense for keeping track of costs on the WindSailor. So my team and I figured out what we needed to know and kept track of that."

"And what about Ralph?" Jenny asked.

I smiled. "That's the funny part. We just reported to him by summarizing our information into what we thought was a simple, useful format. Apparently Ralph thought the same thing, because he never complained. And when we did the project review last week, he commented that the costing reporting was especially well done."

"I don't see the problem, then, Will. Obviously you figured out a better way of doing costing. Why not specify your procedure in the manual?"

I sighed. "That's just it, Jen. I did find a better way—for this project. Maybe in a different project the earned value stuff would be useful. I think that what I'm getting at is that the requirements of each assignment should determine a lot of the detailed procedures. If you try and specify them and make them law, they would have to be as generic as possible, so they would fit all situations. In the process, you would make it so they'd fit no situation."

"Are you saying everyone should start from scratch every time? I don't know if I can agree with that. Think of all the effort required to reinvent the wheel over and over again."

One of the many things that I like about my wife is her ability to make me clarify my thoughts. "I think I have to move upstream of the detailed procedures, and not even try and specify them, if I want to produce something useful."

Jenny nodded. "So why not write something that covers only the fundamentals and leaves the details to the individual project manager?"

"Yeah, but is the world ready to work from first principles and let the situation determine the details? I guess that's what I'm really wrestling with. The fundamental steps will take only a page or two, but I get the feeling that Ralph is expecting a lot more."

I finished drying the dishes with Jenny and went outside to play with the kids. It was a relatively simple (for me) game of monkey in the middle, so I devoted the part of my brain that wasn't working on catching the ball to thinking about the problems that Jenny had helped me articulate:

1. All assignments were governed by some fundamental principles, but they were all different beyond a certain level of detail. A detailed procedure manual would be boring, unread, and worst of all, wrong for most situations.
2. Ralph was expecting a boring, detailed procedure manual on how to do projects at Hyler.
3. People might not be ready to work from fundamental or "first" principles. Some teams might prefer to have a "recipe" book that didn't require them to figure out a lot of things on their own.

Just for fun I threw in:

4. How did I know that I was at the most fundamental level of principles for an assignment? Maybe what I thought of as first principles were still too specific.

Just then something hit me. It was the ball. "Daddy," Jake yelled, "you have to watch. Now you're the monkey."

Later, I took a moment to jot down my difficulties so I could stare at them all at once instead of having to think about them one at a time.

The fourth one turned out to be the one I disposed of first. The most fundamental principles I knew had worked for me. I wouldn't rule out more fundamental things, but would go with what I had. Scratch one problem.

Next I tackled Ralph's expectations. I decided that my success on this assignment had earned me some respect for my ideas. If what I came up with did not exactly fit with his expectations, I hoped he would at least be willing to listen.

I looked at number one. If I believed this, all the effort I would have to put into writing detailed procedures would be mostly wasted, unappreciated by most people, and resented by those who actually read my manual, had to do projects by it, and found it to be wrong.

That left only problem number three: Were people ready to work from first principles instead of detailed procedures? Was it right to let people do the wrong thing because they wanted to? Clearly, I had to try and help them.

So what was the best way to get people to think out their own detailed procedures? As I chewed on my pencil it occurred to me. Why not offer myself as a coach to other people around Hyler who were working on assignments? Why not try and help them in the same way that Martha helped me? (They, of course, would not have to put up with pipe smoking and sarcasm). Time wouldn't be a problem. The time Martha had spent with me over the past year, long as it had seemed, could be counted in hours not days. I could certainly afford that.

I could provide a simple framework of general steps in an assignment, and then coach people to help them with the specific details. I turned on the computer and started to write.

This is a Manual?

"Gee, Will, a whole two pages? I can certainly see why it took you three weeks." I think Stu must have been reading books about leadership in the nineties, because he was trying to change his leadership style from military, to positive consensus building via sarcasm. I had liked him better the old way.

"Stu, give me a chance to explain. I realize it's not exactly what you and Ralph were expecting."

Stu shook his head. "After the tricks you pulled off with the WindSailor, I'm really not surprised. However, Ralph may not be too pleased."

"That's why I'm showing it to you first. I wanted to pre-test the idea."

Patiently, I went into my little song and dance to explain how I had arrived at the two-page procedure manual. As I talked, Stu interrupted occasionally with questions. At the end I asked him, "Well, what do you think? Will Ralph buy it?"

Stu leaned back in his chair and stared up at the ceiling. Then he sat forward. "I don't think so." My face fell. "You should have seen the struggles I had with him during the WindSailor assignment. Whenever things weren't like Al Burton would have done them, Ralph wanted to get on your case. I managed to keep him from doing anything rash, and you came through every time."

"He trusted you before and it worked," I interrupted. "So why won't he buy this?"

"A guy like Ralph can only stray so far from the organizationally accepted norm," he said, holding up his hand to stop me from interrupting again. "I know it made him look successful this time, but the fact is, it's almost always safer to do what everyone else is doing, whatever the flavor of the day may be. And for a guy like Ralph, who wants to get ahead in the corporation, that's the path he'll follow. It's always worked for him in the past. He wants a substantial manual that he can point at when Henry Stanton, president of Mantec, tours the place. Ralph wants the bible on project management. And in case you haven't looked lately, Will, the bible has a lot more than two pages."

I had been slouching lower and lower in my chair. After Stu finished there was silence. Finally I said, "Well, I guess I better get writing." I stood up to leave.

"You know," said Stu, staring at the ceiling again, "I've always been a great fan of Socrates,"

"Really?"

"Yes." He cracked his knuckles. "Ralph wouldn't like your ideas about working from first principles, and coaching others by asking them questions and letting them discover things for themselves, but I do."

"I suppose it reminds you of the good old days when Socrates taught you in high school. Did you have him in grade nine or ten?"

Stu just smiled.

I looked back. "I give up, Stu, why are you telling me about Socrates?"

"No particular reason, Will. It's just that as the new president of Hyler, you might find me a little more open to your ideas than Ralph was."

I stared at him. "You're kidding me."

Stu shook his head. I gave a war cry and jumped over his desk to shake his hand. Unfortunately I caught my toe on his phone and ended up in his lap. He didn't seem to mind.

Stu was all smiles. "The WindSailor really was Ralph's ticket out of here to bigger and better things. As of September 1, you can call me Mr. President."

True to his word, Stu was very receptive to my first principles document, and it has become Hyler's standard for managing assignments. It looks like this:

The Survival Manual for Project Managers

Structure of an Assignment:

GENESIS
DESIGN
EXECUTION PLAN (Project)
EXECUTION
REVIEW
    1. (Review of Design)
    2. (Review of Execution Plan and Execution)
    3. (Review of Genesis)

When asked to do an Assignment:

1. **Identify the sponsor.** He or she is the person who can spend the money.
2. **Make sure the sponsor knows who the sponsor is.** The sponsor must understand his/her responsibilities. This should be part of the culture, but never assume.

3. **Write the first objective statement**. Make sure you answer *all* of these questions:
   - What is wrong with the existing situation?
   - How will things be better when we are done?
   - What are the performance criteria for the deliverables?
   - What is the scope of the assignment (i.e., what is in the assignment and what is not in the assignment)?
   - What are the specific constraints regarding cost, time, quality, and so on?
   - Who is the sponsor?
   - Who is the project manager?
   - What authority is being given?

4. **Have the sponsor sign the objective statement**. Always get a signature on the document.

5. **Collect the best project team that you can**. Remember, the same responsibilities must be fulfilled on every assignment, but team members may double up on some roles depending on the assignment. After sponsor and project manager, roles include: feasibility analyst, designer, user's rep, project administrator, implementer.

6. **Create the conceptual design**.

7. **Get the sponsor's signed approval of both the conceptual design and the funding to complete the detailed design**.

8. **Detail the design**. You'll know it's complete if you can do an execution plan.

9. **Get the sponsor's signature on the detailed design**.

10. **Create the execution plan with the project team**. Use the logic of the interrelation of the activities to create a dependency chart, which will be the basis for determining things like costs, schedule, and resource requirements.

11. **Get the sponsor's signature on the execution plan**.

12. **Execute the plan**.

13. **Review the assignment**. Complete all three review steps.

Part Eight

New Frameworks

24

Checking Assumptions

The elm-lined trees of Darfield worked their usual magic as I drove to my in-laws' house. During the past year, in my distracted state of mind, I failed to notice the regal splendor of the old trees and the beautiful old houses. Today was different. I purposefully took my time, drinking in the exquisite visual.

"Hey, mister, watch where you're going!" I jerked the steering wheel to the left, barely avoiding a twelve year-old on a skateboard. "You been drinking, buddy? Or just learning to drive?" I thought I had been a little more polite when I was twelve. Or maybe this guy was a 30 year old midget with an attitude.

"Daddy, you should be more careful," Sarah said solemnly. She had asked to come along with me to visit her great-grandmother.

I quickly drove the remainder of Elm Street to Fred and Natalie's place and pulled into the driveway. I had intended this trip as kind of a thank-you pilgrimage where I would pay homage to Martha's wisdom. It was now August 28, almost a year to the day since I had been tapped for the WindSailor assignment. Demand for our product had continued unabated. By adding extra shifts, we had managed to exceed the most optimistic production estimates, and everyone at Hyler was feeling very good about the prospects for next year and beyond. More important to me, there had been no problems with the production facilities, all of the information systems were operating without glitches, and our new workforce was fitting in well. Realist that I am, I had to give credit where it was really due.

Martha was in her regular place on the porch, rocking in her rocking chair and smoking her pipe. The number of smoke rings hanging in the still air over the flower bed in front of the porch were silent testimony to her on going vigil. For a moment I stopped and admired the tableau. The defiant, crotchety, yet wise old woman with her rocking chair and pipe, was undoubtedly thinking deep thoughts about important management issues. "Well, it's about time you came to visit, Willie! No problems for a while, eh? No need for old Martha to kick around." When she saw Sarah her tone changed. "Hi, honey, come on up."

Sarah ran up the stairs to Martha, and I followed. "I wanted to thank you for all the help you provided me on the WindSailor assignment. Everything has been a big success, and it's all thanks to you. And as a token of my appreciation, I got you a little gift." I held out the box. "Here."

Sarah was on Martha's lap by this time. "You go off and see your grandmother, Sarah. Your dad and I have to talk." Sarah jumped down and banged through the screen door into the house.

As she eyed the gift in my outstretched hand, I could tell she was pleased, but in true Martha fashion she said crustily. "There isn't much I need at my age. I'll be dead soon, anyway." So saying, she tore off the wrapping paper eagerly.

Inside was a tin of high-grade Turkish pipe tobacco. After a lot of research—and over the objections of Jenny, who didn't think Martha needed any more help killing herself—I had hunted down this tin of what was supposed to be a pipe smoker's paradise. "Good brand," was all Martha said, and I didn't expect more.

I sat down in the chair beside her. "To be honest, Martha, I also wanted to ask you a few questions. Some things are still puzzling me."

"Just a few questions?" Martha gave me a glance that seemed to say someone as dumb as me should have more than just a few questions.

I ignored the look. "There were some things Ralph talked about at the beginning of the project. Total Quality Management stuff, and the self-directed work teams, not to mention things like earned value costing and work breakdown structures. I avoided them, because I've always had bad experiences with those things. But inside I worried that I was missing the boat. I know we never had a problem with quality. We worked well as a team. We didn't need earned value costing or work breakdown structures. We just did what worked." I paused.

"So?" prompted Martha, "What's your problem?"

"I guess the problem is, everybody at the company likes the job we did. So why don't we just implement 'management by projects' at Hyler and get rid of all of that other crap?"

"People are funny, Will. If you ask someone to drive nails with his bare hands, he'll get frustrated real quickly. The human hand isn't a very good tool for driving nails. Give them a hammer, they're happy as a pig in—. They'll drive nails like there's no tomorrow. The only problem is that pretty soon everything starts looking like a nail. Everything you ask them to do, they try and do it with a hammer because it works so well for driving nails. Of course not everything is a nail."

I could see her point. "Not everything is an assignment, or a project. Trying to force everything into that framework means trouble."

Martha smiled. "Exactly."

"What about Total Quality Management then? It seems to be all-pervasive."

"Have you ever heard of the Bentskin Award?"

"Sure. It's an award given every year to a company that demonstrates significant improvement in, and devotion to, the quality of their product." I thought that sounded pretty extensive, considering I really didn't know all that much about it.

"Close enough," Martha told me. "And if a company wins this award, what would you imagine some of the company's characteristics might be?"

There was a trap somewhere, but I figured it was best to just soldier on. Give the old gal her fun.

"Well," I began, "a company that won this award would likely be a leader in its particular niche, would be highly profitable, have happy employees, and maybe have been saved on the brink of disaster by the introduction of this total quality stuff. Maybe it would be a real turnaround story."

She smiled in her shark-like manner, which told me I had guessed wrong—as usual. "What would you say," she asked me, "if I told you that more than 60 percent of the companies that have won that award, filed for Chapter 11 bankruptcy protection within eighteen months of the ceremony?"

Part of me could well believe it. "Look," I said finally, "you know something here."

She explained patiently, "The best way for you to know it is to figure it out."

Defining Quality

It seemed to me that if these quality award winners were going under shortly after reaching the pinnacle of success, there were three possibilities.

First, the guidelines for choosing the winners must be fuzzy if companies that won weren't really achieving the quality they claimed.

Second, perhaps companies that were into quality in a big way were in high-risk sectors, susceptible to downturns in the economy. When things got bad, poof, they went under. This seemed even less probable than the first possibility.

Third, they were using the same tool to fix everything. That meant they were using the wrong tool most of the time.

That's what I told Martha.

"You haven't got to the heart of the problem. For starters, what is quality?"

"Excellence," I said without hesitation.

"What is excellence?" she rejoined with no hesitation herself.

"Well," I said, stalling for a second, "good, better than the rest."

"What is good?"

Damn, I thought, this was how all of the project stuff started. "What," I said, "is the point of all of these definitions?"

Martha delivered a stare that said I was getting out of line. I thought for a moment. "I don't know, good is not bad. How's that?"

This seemed to perk the old girl right up. "You're right, you don't really understand what the words *quality* and *excellence* mean. You might understand the definitions, but you haven't thought carefully about what they mean." She settled back in her rocker.

"You did define quality correctly. Excellence is usually the fourth or fifth definition. The first definition has to do with characteristics that make something what it is—its attributes. The degree of excellence that a thing possesses implies some judgement about the thing. In other words, someone has decided that the combination of qualities a thing possesses is excellent or superior. But there is a characteristic of this definition that you need to understand in order to use the word effectively. I've given you all the clues."

Martha finished up her pipe-lighting procedure while she waited.

I just sat there stupid. Again I resigned myself to thinking. What was it about the word quality, or even apparently, the word excellence? What was the key characteristic? Nothing came to mind. "I need to take a little stroll to the washroom. I'll be back in five minutes."

"Take your time, Willie. And don't worry, the answer won't go anywhere either. That's the beauty of first principles—they're always around."

I headed inside, straight towards all of the reference books that Natalie and Fred kept on the bookshelf in their living room. This included several dictionaries. I took a moment to look up some words.

Sure enough, *quality* was just as Martha defined it. The first definition was "the attributes or characteristics of a thing." It wasn't until the third definition that the word *excellence* came into it. Dead end. I looked up *excellence*. As expected: "Superior, surpassing goodness." It sounded like little boys in Sunday School and it didn't shed any light. *Good* was little help either. The definition included the word *excellence*! *Good* was one of largest entries in the dictionary.

I decided to take the radical, underworld track and look up the word *Bad*.

Bad was defined as "a lack of goodness," and I felt like tearing out my hair. Interestingly, bad was also defined as "lacking in quality" and "defective." The two were obviously connected.

Finally, it dawned on me. Something can be excellent only in relation to something else, even it's only a person's expectation. And therefore for something to be quality, the way it is used in Total Quality Management, there had to be some kind of comparison. *Quality* is a relative term.

I rushed back out to the porch, paused at the door to catch my breath and put on a nonchalant exterior, and strolled out looking, I thought, like a man who had worked it out for himself.

"Any luck with the dictionary?" Martha asked.

"In fact," I said, attempting to maintain my worldly exterior, "I think I did have some luck. The key quality of quality—" I smiled at my cleverness, "is that when it means excellence or superiority, it's a relative term."

"Well, well," said Martha, "you surprise me every time. You're right. The word quality is frequently used today to mean the characteristic of excellence. And when it is used in that fashion, it is a relative term. So what does Total Quality Management mean?"

That was easy. "Total Good Management, relative to everyone else, or to how the company was in the past."

"Pretty vague isn't it? Now, what do you suppose managers were doing before TQM came along?" She watched me to see if I could continue my success.

"Before TQM, most companies were probably trying to do a good job."

"So what would TQM do for them?"

"Nothing. At Hyler, it actually made things worse."

Martha sighed. "A technique called Statistical Quality Control, which essentially involved using statistics to help improve manufacturing operations, gained enormous popularity in Japan in the fifties. Many management gurus attributed Japan's comeback from the ruin of the war to the use of SQC. By the time Japan was outperforming North America, the hammer had been found: Its name was Quality Control. Ironically, most of the people who attempt to apply TQM today weren't even with us in Japan."

"You were in Japan?"

"That's another story, Will. The point is, a great deal of harm has come from applying that particular hammer to every situational nail."

"And when it doesn't work, it mutates into many different, fuzzy, forms." I added.

"And it hasn't been a pretty sight."

Other Techniques

We sat in silence for a few moments as we contemplated the implications of the misapplication of hammers. Finally, Martha said, "What do you think about managing your company entirely by projects?"

I thought a lot differently. "I think the techniques you taught me should be applied only to things that truly are assignments. Project management is not the universal tool. But to be honest, Martha, I'm having trouble. What processes don't fit into the framework of an assignment?"

"Many things, Will. The strategic planning process, production control, performance management, just to name a few. The techniques that we've talked about over the last year are merely one small but important set of the management tools available for improving the overall situation. Don't think that you know it all yet!"

Then Martha grunted and slowly got up off her rocker. "I'm glad the WindSailor worked out, Will. Old as I am, I still get quite a thrill out of helping somebody out. But all this talking has made me tired. Why don't you get off home and feed my great-granddaughter. Pretty selfish of you to keep her here past dinner time! Come see me next time you have a problem." That was Martha, crusty to the end.

I left with a lot on my mind, but very little of it had to do with projects.

The End

Epilogue

In a novel, it is permissible to introduce elements of luck and coincidence that would be out of place in other forms of communication. So it is with *Making it Happen*. Although the characters in this book are drawn from real life, happy endings are often elusive.

That is largely because the necessary support sometimes does not come together in the right time and place. The rarity of real life characters like Stu Barnes is remarkable. Organizations often lack the will, as much or more so, than the tools and techniques required to succeed.

Manageering Associates has developed a number of tools to help organizations improve how projects are managed, and the author welcomes inquiries.

He can be contacted at:
> Phone:(250) 479-5553
> email: mkyle@direct.ca